D1076724

50 Walks in
STAFFORDSHIRE

Produced by AA Publishing
© AA Media Limited 2013

First published 2003
Second edition 2009
New edition 2013

Published by AA Publishing (a trading name of AA Media Limited, whose registered office is Fanum House, Basing View, Basingstoke, Hampshire RG21 4EA; registered number 06112600)

Researched and written by Paul Grogan, Hugh Taylor and Moira McCrossan
Field checked and updated 2013 by Andrew McCloy and Ronald Turnbull

Series Management: David Popey
Editor: Karen Kemp
Designer: Tracey Butler
Proofreader: Ann F Stonehouse
Digital imaging & repro: Ian Little
Cartography provided by the Mapping Services Department of AA Publishing

Printed and bound in the UK by Butler, Tanner & Dennis

Mapping in this book is derived from the following products:
OS Landranger 118 (walks 3–16, 20, 25)
OS Landranger 119 (walks 1–4, 8, 9, 13, 14, 17–24)
OS Landranger 127 (walks 25–29, 32–35, 41)
OS Landranger 128 (walks 30, 31, 33, 34, 36, 37)
OS Landranger 138 (walks 46, 48–50)
OS Landranger 139 (walks 43–47)
OS Explorer 244 (walks 38–40)
Contains Ordnance Survey data
© Crown copyright and database right 2013 Ordnance Survey. Licence number 100021153.

A05038

ISBN: 978-0-7495-7486-4
ISBN (SS): 978-0-7495-7512-0

A CIP catalogue record for this book is available from the British Library.

The Automobile Association would like to thank the following photographers, companies and picture libraries for their assistance in the preparation of this book. Abbreviations for the picture credits are as follows: (t) top; (b) bottom; (l) left; (r) right; (AA) AA World Travel Library.

3 AA/T Mackie; 9 AA/C Jones; 10 AA/C Jones; 12/13 AA/C Jones; 24/25 AA/T Mackie; 32/33 AA/J Welsh; 40/41 AA/T Mackie; 56/57 AA/C Jones; 74/75 AA/C Jones; 92/93 AA/C Jones; 130 AA/C Jones; 137 AA/C Jones; 154/155 AA/C Jones

Every effort has been made to trace the copyright holders, and we apologise in advance for any accidental errors. We would be happy to apply the corrections in the following edition of this publication.

Some of the walks may appear in other AA books and publications.

Visit AA Publishing at theAA.com/shop

Right: The Roaches (Walk 3)

50 Walks in
STAFFORDSHIRE

50 Walks of 2–10 Miles

Contents

The Walks

Following the Walks

An information panel for each walk shows its relative difficulty, the distance and total amount of ascent. An indication of the gradients you will encounter is shown by the rating ▲▲▲ (no steep slopes) to ▲▲▲ (several very steep slopes). Each walk is rated for its relative difficulty compared to the other walks in this book. Walks marked +++ and colour-coded green are likely to be shorter and easier with little total ascent. Those marked with +++ and colour-coded orange are of intermediate difficulty. The hardest walks are marked +++ and colour-coded red.

MAPS

There are 40 maps, covering the 50 walks. Some walks have a suggested option in the same area. The information panel for these walks will tell you how much extra walking is involved. On short-cut suggestions the panel will tell you the total distance if you set out from the start of the main walk. Where an option returns to the same point on the main walk, just the distance of the loop is given. Where an option leaves the main walk at one point and returns to it at another, then the distance shown is for the whole walk. The minimum time suggested is for reasonably fit walkers and doesn't allow for stops. Each walk has a suggested map.

ROUTE MAP LEGEND

– –➔– –	Walk Route	▭	Built-up Area
❶	Route Waypoint	▬	Woodland Area
– – – –	Adjoining Path	🚻	Toilet
＼＼⁄⁄	Viewpoint	**P**	Car Park
•	Place of Interest	⊞	Picnic Area
⌒	Steep Section	)(	Bridge

START POINTS

The start of each walk is given as a six-figure grid reference prefixed by two letters indicating which 100km square of the National Grid it refers to. You'll find more information on grid references on most Ordnance Survey, AA Walking and Leisure Maps.

DOGS

We have tried to give dog owners useful advice about how dog friendly each walk is. Please respect other countryside users. Keep your dog under control, especially around livestock, and obey local bylaws and other dog control notices.

CAR PARKING

Many of the car parks suggested are public, but occasionally you may find you have to park on the roadside or in a lay-by. Please be considerate when you leave your car, ensuring that access roads or gates are not blocked and that other vehicles can pass safely.

WALKS LOCATOR

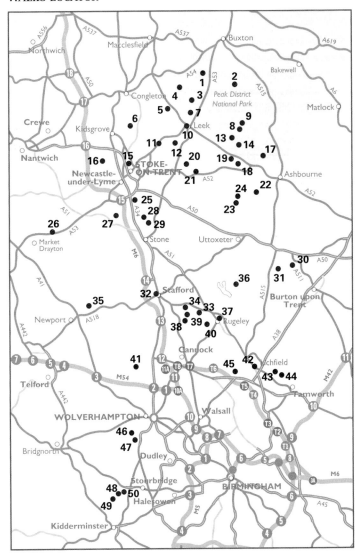

Walking in Staffordshire

Did you know that Staffordshire bore the brunt of the largest non-nuclear explosion of World War II? Or that the county's regiment once boasted within its ranks the most decorated NCO of World War I? Or going back a little further, that George Handel penned his masterpiece, *The Messiah*, on Staffordshire soil? If so, you'll no doubt also be aware that Staffordshire was home to the first canals and the first factory in Britain, that it had front-row seats for the drama surrounding one of the most notorious murder trials of the 19th century, and – more recently – that it provided the scenery and setting for the slightly less macabre television drama *Peak Practice*.

But even the most well versed of Staffordshire aficionados should still be able to find a few novel nuggets in this little volume, if not to entertain and amuse, then at least to inform and educate. Of course, the county's varied culture and interesting history are all well and good, but what of its potential for walking?

In outline, Staffordshire looks not unlike the profile of a man giving Leicestershire a big kiss (have a look if you don't believe it!). The man's forehead to the northeast of the county is arguably the best region for hillwalking as it comprises a significant chunk of the Peak District. This area is characterised by lofty moors, deep dales and tremendous views of both. In fact seven of the walks can be found in this area, from the great crags of the Roaches to the mysterious Thor's Cave. Further south, at around ear level, are the six sprawling towns that make up Stoke-on-Trent, which historically have had such an impact on Staffordshire's fortunes, not to mention its culture and countryside. This is pottery country, formerly at the forefront of the Industrial Revolution and the driving force behind a network of canals that still criss-crosses the county.

In terms of its scenery, the region around Stoke is surprisingly hilly, thanks largely to vast outcrops of limestone not unlike those found in the Peak District just to the north. In areas where industry once marched rampant o'er hill and down dale, mother nature has recently re-staked her claim on the landscape, which today is typified by peaceful wooded valleys, pond-pearled streams and gently rolling hills.

Next up, hanging like an earring from the lobe of Stoke, is Stafford, home to one of the oldest and most impressive castle earthworks in the country. In fact, glancing at some of the other walks in this area, you'd be forgiven for thinking that it's always been a region of conflict, what with the bloody battlefield of Bloreheath just to the west and the enormous Fauld Crater just to the east.

Just to the south of Stafford is Cannock Chase, arguably the county's best-kept secret. Here, acre after acre of ancient hunting forest has been reclaimed from the devastation wrought by industry to form

Right: Lichfield Cathedral (Walk 42)

a huge forested nature park, just a stone's throw from Birmingham. It would take you days, if not weeks, to walk every track in these justifiably popular woods.

And finally, at the southern tip of the county, along the back of our man's neck, are the slopes and ridges that terminate in the impressive vantage point of Kinver Edge, where entire houses are carved into the sandstone cliffs, and where the fine English wine, in a good year, flows freely. Of course, for walking, any year is a good year in Staffordshire.

PUBLIC TRANSPORT Staffordshire is very well served by public transport: First PMT (08708 500868) is one of the main operators in the northeast of the county, while Arriva (www.arrivabus.co.uk) services routes throughout the region. Local bus timetables for most major towns and routes can be obtained from Traveline (0871 200 22 33 or www.traveline.org.uk). To plan your journey online go to www.transportdirect.info.

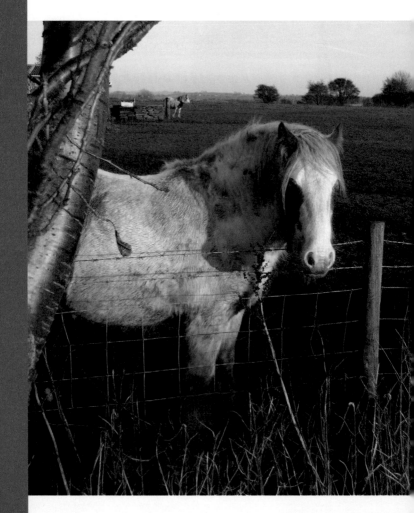

Above: Horses at Wardlow (Walk 18)

Walking in Safety

All these walks are suitable for any reasonably fit person, but less experienced walkers should try the easier walks first. Route finding is usually straightforward, but you will find that an Ordnance Survey or AA walking map is a useful addition to the route maps and descriptions; recommendations can be found in the information panels.

RISKS

Although each walk here has been researched with a view to minimising the risks to the walkers who follow its route, no walk in the countryside can be considered to be completely free from risk. Walking in the outdoors will always require a degree of common sense and judgement to ensure that it is as safe as possible.

- Be particularly careful on cliff paths and in upland terrain, where the consequences of a slip can be very serious.
- Remember to check tidal conditions before walking on the seashore.
- Some sections of route are by, or cross, busy roads. Take care and remember traffic is a danger even on minor country lanes.
- Be careful around farmyard machinery and livestock, especially if you have children with you.
- Be aware of the consequences of changes in the weather and check the forecast before you set out. Carry spare clothing and a torch if you are walking in the winter months. Remember the weather can change very quickly at any time of the year, and in moorland and heathland areas, mist and fog can make route finding much harder. Don't set out in these conditions unless you are confident of your navigation skills in poor visibility. In summer remember to take account of the heat and sun; wear a hat and carry water.
- On walks away from centres of population you should carry a whistle and survival bag. If you do have an accident requiring the emergency services, make a note of your position as accurately as possible and dial 999.

COUNTRYSIDE CODE
- Be safe, plan ahead and follow any signs.
- Leave gates and property as you find them.
- Protect plants and animals and take your litter home.
- Keep dogs under close control.
- Consider other people.

For more information visit www.naturalengland.org.uk/ourwork/ enjoying/countrysidecode

Overleaf: The moors above Flash (Walk 1)

The High Village of Flash

DISTANCE 6 miles (9.7km)	**MINIMUM TIME** 3hrs 30min
ASCENT/GRADIENT 1,200ft (365m) ▲▲▲	**LEVEL OF DIFFICULTY** ✚✚✚

PATHS Field and moorland paths, can be boggy after rain, some roads, many stiles

LANDSCAPE Hills, moorland and meadows

SUGGESTED MAP AA Walker's Map 1 Central Peak District

START/FINISH Grid reference: SK026672

DOG FRIENDLINESS Suitable for dogs, but keep on lead near livestock

PARKING On roadside in village

PUBLIC TOILETS None on route

At an altitude of 1,518ft (463m), Flash proclaims itself the 'Highest Village in Britain'. At this elevation, winters come early and linger long. Once, during wartime, it got so cold that the vicar had icicles on his ears when he reached the church. On another occasion a visiting minister arrived by motorcycle, much to the astonishment of the congregation because heavy snow was imminent. They told him to watch the window opposite his pulpit and should he see it falling, he should stop the service and depart. Just after he left, it started to snow and within 20 minutes the village was cut off.

SHARP PRACTICE

Despite being a devout community, Flash also has the dubious honour of giving its name to sharp practice, with the terms 'flash money' and 'flash company'. A group of peddlers living near the village travelled the country hawking ribbons, buttons and goods made in nearby Leek. Known as 'Flash men' they initially paid for their goods with hard cash, but after establishing credit vanished with the goods and moved on to another supplier. Their name became associated with ne'er-do-wells in taverns, who helped people drink their money and were never seen again, as typified in the 18th-century English folk-song, *Flash Company*:

Fiddling and dancing were all my delight
But keeping flash company has ruined me quite...

BEYOND THE LAW

'Flash money', on the other hand, referred to counterfeit bank notes, manufactured in the 18th century by a devious local gang using button presses. They were captured when a servant girl told the authorities. Some of the gang members were hanged at Chester. Flash was the ideal location for avoiding the law because of its proximity to the borders of three counties – police in one county could not pursue miscreants into another. At a local beauty spot called Three Shire Heads, about a mile (1.6km) northwest of the village, by a packhorse bridge, is the meeting place of Derbyshire, Cheshire and Staffordshire. Illegal bare-knuckle fights were held here and when the police arrived, the participants simply crossed the bridge and continued their bout on the other side. While all this lawlessness was going on the more peaceable inhabitants formed the Tea Pot Club. Originally a fund to help members who were sick, the Flash Loyal Union Society still has an annual Tea Pot Parade each June from the church to Flash Bar.

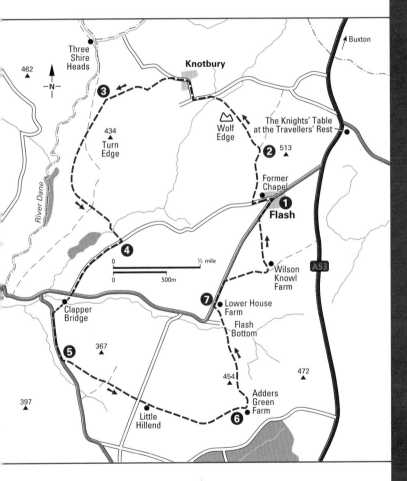

❶ Walk into the village and bear right past the pub. After 100yds (91m), branch right on a track. Beyond the last cottage, turn off right to head away across three fields. Meeting a walled track, go right. Beyond a stile,

walk on to go through a gate in the left wall.

❷ At the track's end, bear right over Wolf Edge. Beyond a redundant stile, descend beside the right boundary.

A short way along, slip across, but revert back over a lower stile. A faint path angles down to a lane. Go left, then right into Knotbury. After the last house, leave at a fingerpost on the left. Head downhill beside the wall. Ignoring a crossing, continue with the moorland path onto Turn Edge.

❸ Over the crest, descend left, passing through trees to a track. Go left for 100yds (91m), then branch off at a waypost, along another falling track. Maintain a slant across rough enclosures to a gravel track. Walk left to a waypost, leaving on a bend for a grassy path straight ahead (not down across the rough slope to the right). Cross a stile and keep ahead, the way eventually steepening into a deep valley. As the track drops towards the stream, it zig-zags to meet a ford to the right. The footbridge is straight ahead, hidden by gorse, but a wooden pole supporting a power cable is a guide to locate it. Climb uphill to the lane at Spring Head.

❹ Turn right. At the junction, go right and immediately left through a gap. Go downhill through scrub to a clapper bridge. Head up and left across a field to a lane. Follow it uphill.

❺ After 0.25 miles (400m), leave left through a squeeze gap. Cross a pasture, then follow a faint path across moorland grazing. Beyond a building go ahead to reach a lane, cross it and continue opposite beside Little Hillend. A distinct, rough path leads onto the moor, eventually crossing a track from Ann Roach Farm. Go over a stile, through a gate and turn right to Adders Green Farm.

❻ At the entrance, go left through a gate. Follow the left wall at its corner to another gate. Bear right below a rise, the path soon descending to Flash Bottom. Drop off the moor through a plantation to a footbridge and walk left to a drive.

❼ Go through a gate opposite, follow the path over a field and up steps to the road. Turn uphill, then leave right after 200yds (183m) at a stile. Bear left towards a farm. Cross a bridge and stile below a power post, climb away left, heading back across the fields to the lane. Emerging left of the 'Flash' sign, continue up to the village.

WHERE TO EAT AND DRINK The Knights' Table at the Travellers' Rest in Flash Bar is the best place in the area. Walkers can be assured of a warm welcome and can relax in front of a fire with a pint of real ale, enjoying the ambience of this fine old building with its flag floors and oak beams.

WHAT TO SEE Look for evidence of the network of packhorse trails on the moors. These routes were used from medieval times to transport goods between communities. Packhorse trains could have anything up to 50 horses and were led by a man called a 'jagger' (their ponies were Galloway cross-breeds called Jaegers). Today you will find their paved routes, descending into the valleys in distinctive 'hollow ways' or sunken lanes.

WHILE YOU'RE THERE Visit Buxton, England's highest market town. Founded by the Romans after they discovered a hot spring in AD 79, it became a spa town in the 18th century. The elegant Crescent is modelled on Bath's Royal Crescent and the street fountain here is still fed from St Ann's Well. There are many fine buildings, and the Pavilion Gardens, with an iron-and-glass pavilion fronted by formal gardens, are not to be missed.

Around Longnor

DISTANCE 6 miles (9.7km)   MINIMUM TIME 3hrs 30min

ASCENT/GRADIENT 459ft (140m) ▲▲▲   LEVEL OF DIFFICULTY ✦✦✦

PATHS Some on road, otherwise good footpaths, can be muddy, many stiles

LANDSCAPE Valleys, hills and meadows

SUGGESTED MAP AA Walker's Map 1 Central Peak District

START/FINISH Grid reference: SK089649

DOG FRIENDLINESS Suitable for dogs, but keep on lead near livestock

PARKING Longnor village square

PUBLIC TOILETS Longnor village square

Longnor, a charming Peak village situated on a high ridge between the Dove and Manifold rivers, developed as a meeting place on the ancient trade routes that once crossed these hills from Sheffield, Chesterfield, Nottingham and the Potteries. In 1993 it became famous as the location of the television drama *Peak Practice*, which chronicled the everyday lives of a group of country doctors and their patients. Earlier episodes took many different parts of the area to establish fictional Cardale – particularly Crich. However, the drama finally established a base in this little Staffordshire village to give the programmes a more permanent, community feel. It ceased filming in 2002.

FAMILIAR PLACES

There is plenty that will be familiar to viewers of *Peak Practice*. The fine brick frontage of the fictional Cardale Tearoom is actually a Georgian hotel built to serve the needs of the Crewe and Harpur Estate, and still retains that name. It was used as a meeting place for the local farmers when they came to pay their annual rents at the end of March. The Horseshoe had the honour of being the TV doctors' local, the Black Swan. Dating back to 1609, it was an important staging point for the packhorse and carriage trade that crossed these hills. Ye Olde Cheshire Cheese, one of two other pubs in the village, had its origins as a cheese store in 1464. It still has a reputation for fine food, but its main attraction is its resident ghost, Mrs Robins, a former tenant.

The ancient pubs and market square are a reminder of Longnor's importance as a market town. The turnpike roads with their tolls, and the lack of a railway link, prevented Longnor's development as a major trading centre, but the village retains its Victorian market hall. Now a craft centre and coffee shop, it still has the old market toll charge board, with a list of long-forgotten tariffs, above the front door. However, Longnor's old world ambience and location at the heart of ancient paths ensures that it is still busy with walkers, cyclists and tourists.

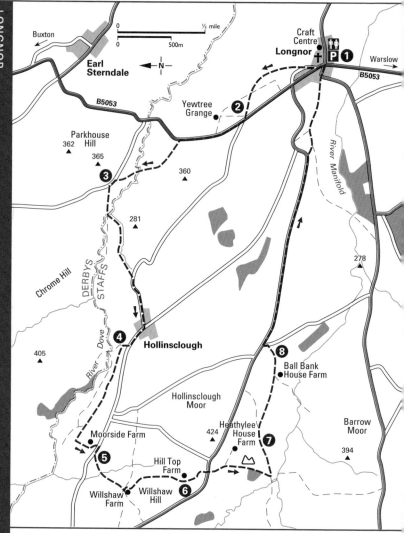

❶ From the square take the road towards Buxton. Take the first right to turn into Church Street, then go immediately left up Lane Head and right up steps to the footpath. Follow the waymarkers, behind some houses, over a stile and along a wall. Cross another stile, go downhill and turn left onto a farm road.

❷ Go straight on and turn right onto the road. Just before the bend towards the bottom of the hill, take the farm road on the left. At the end, continue through a gate onto the footpath, through a gap stile, downhill, across a bridge and continue straight ahead. Eventually go through a gate and turn left onto the road.

❸ Fork left onto a farm road, following the waymarked path. Cross a bridge by a ford and turn left to follow the river bank to the road. Turn right through Hollinsclough, following the road to the right and uphill. Turn right onto a bridleway, go through a gate and downhill.

4 After 50yds (46m) fork left by two stones and continue along the flank of the hill. Cross a stile and continue until the path meets a stone wall, then veer left and uphill. At the top turn left at a stone gatepost, and walk through Moorside Farm and through a kissing gate to the road. Turn right, then cross a stile to a public footpath on the left.

5 Follow a line downhill from the fingerpost, aiming for the gate in the field beyond the trees and the brook. In very wet weather this is a quagmire. Cross a stile and the brook and head uphill, through a gap in the wall by a gate at the top, and turn left through Willshaw Farm. Fork right for the well-signposted path to Hill Top Farm.

6 Follow the path over stiles and past the farm to the road. Go straight over for the track signposted

'Heathylee House Farm'. Approaching the farm go right, steeply downhill, over a stile and follow the path along the wall. Just before the stream, cross a stile on the left and head uphill to the left of some trees.

7 Continue walking uphill, through a gate in a stone wall to a ruined building. Follow the track to the next farm, bear left after the barn, then go left onto a footpath uphill.

8 Go through a stile and follow the wall uphill to the road. Turn left, then right towards Longnor. Just as the road bends left, cross a stile on the right, go downhill and over several stiles and gates to a farm road. Turn right and follow this road back to the village and your car.

WHERE TO EAT AND DRINK Longnor has plenty of places. The Manifold Tea Room and Take Away is a traditional fish-and-chip shop with indoor seating. The Craft Centre and Coffee Shop, in the former market hall, serves home-made cakes and cream teas.

WHAT TO SEE Some 350 million years ago, Britain lay south of the equator and the Peak District enjoyed a tropical climate. The Peak limestones were built up over millions of years from the remains of shells, corals and tiny aquatic creatures called crinoids. Parkhouse and Chrome hills, two prominent landmarks on this walk, are limestone reefs that formed, rather like mud or silt piles, during this period.

WHILE YOU'RE THERE Well dressing is a centuries old tradition in this area. A wooden framework holds a bed of clay, into which flower petals, moss, berries, cones and seeds are pressed in an intricate design. The display is then placed over the well in a special ceremony. Each village has its own design and date. Dressings take place throughout the summer.

Lud's Church
and the Roaches

DISTANCE 6.75 miles (10.9km)	**MINIMUM TIME** 3hrs 30min

ASCENT/GRADIENT 1,020ft (311m) ▲▲▲   **LEVEL OF DIFFICULTY** +++

PATHS Rocky moorland paths, forest tracks and road

LANDSCAPE Moor and woodland

SUGGESTED MAP AA Leisure Map 7 Central Peak District

START/FINISH Grid reference: SK003621

DOG FRIENDLINESS Keep on lead near livestock

PARKING In lay-by on lane near Windygates Hall Farm

PUBLIC TOILETS None on route

The jagged ridge of the Roaches is one of the most popular outdoor locations in the Peak District National Park. It was here on the gritstone crags that the 'working class revolution' in climbing took place in the 1950s. Manchester lads Joe Brown and Don Whillans became legends within the climbing fraternity by developing new rock-climbing techniques wearing gym shoes and using a discarded clothes-line as a rope. Other less tangible legends are associated with Doxey Pool. Locals tell of a young mermaid who lived in the pool but was captured by a group of men. It is said her ghost can still be heard singing through the mist. Lurking in the darkest depths of the pool is Jenny Greenteeth, a hideous green monster who grabs the ankles of anyone unfortunate enough to get too close, dragging them to a watery grave.

SIR GAWAIN AND THE GREEN KNIGHT

But the greatest legend associated with the Roaches is the Arthurian tale of Sir Gawain and the Green Knight. According to the 14th-century poem a knight on horseback, cloaked entirely in green, gatecrashed a feast at Camelot and challenged the Knights of the Round Table. Sir Gawain rose to the challenge and beheaded the Green Knight, but the latter retrieved his head and laughingly challenged Sir Gawain to meet with him again, in a year's time, at the Green Chapel. This was identified in the 1950s as Lud's Church, near the Roaches, by Professor Ralph Elliot, now of the University of Adelaide in Australia.

Professor Elliot's theory was supported by a group of linguists working on the poem at the same time, who placed the work in the same 15-mile (24km) radius. The professor and a group of students from Keele University, where he was then based, tramped all over the countryside looking for a suitable cave to match the poetic description, and Lud's Church fitted the bill:

A hole in each end and on either side,
And overgrown with grass and great patches
All hollow it was within, only an old cavern
Or the crevice of an ancient crag.

This rocky cleft was created by a mass of sandstone slipping away
from the slope of the hill. Here Sir Gawain kept his rendezvous with the
Green Knight, who lost his head for a second time.

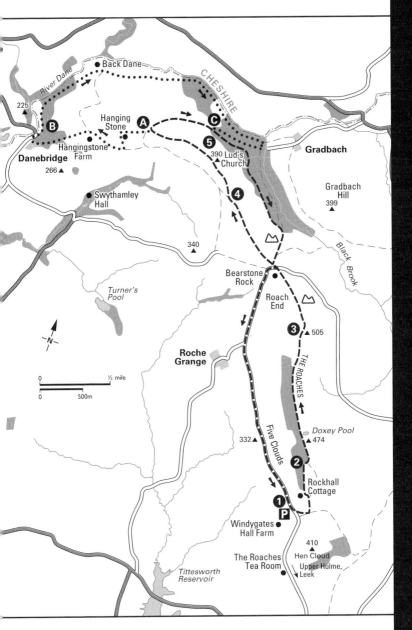

❶ From the lane go through the main gate by the interpretation panel and follow the path half right to the end of the rocks. At a gate in the wall on your right, turn left and go straight uphill on a rocky track. Go left through a pair of stone gateposts and continue right on a well-defined track.

❷ The path is flanked by rocks on the right and woodland to the left and below. Follow it to the right and uphill through a gap in the rocks. Turn left and then continue uphill. Continue following this ridge path. Pass to the left of Doxey Pool and on towards the trig point.

❸ From here descend on a paved path, past the Bearstone Rock, to join the road at Roach End. Go through a gap in the wall, ahead and through a gate and follow the path uphill, keeping the wall on the left. At the signpost fork right onto the concessionary path signposted 'Swythamley via Ridge'.

❹ Follow this path, keeping straight ahead at a crossroads (not right, signed 'Lud's Church'), go through a wall gate and up towards an outcrop. Carry on along the ridge, then head down to a signpost by a gate. Turn right and follow the bridleway signed 'Gradbach and Lud's Church'. At the next signpost fork right towards Lud's Church.

❺ After exploring Lud's Church continue along the path, through woodland, following the signs for the Roaches, eventually taking a paved path uphill. Keep the wall on your left-hand side and at the top, cross a stile onto the gated road. Follow this back to the lay-by near Windygates Hall Farm.

WHERE TO EAT AND DRINK The Roaches Tea Room at Paddock Farm sits beneath the rocky outcrop of Hen Cloud, about 0.6 miles (1km) down the road towards Leek. The food is home-made, excellent and there's plenty of it. There's a conservatory overlooking a herb garden and superb views across Tittesworth Reservoir. It's open daily all year.

WHAT TO SEE Look out for Rockhall Cottage, which is built into the rock and contains at least one room that is a natural cave. This listed building is a former gamekeeper's residence, currently owned by the Peak District National Park. Restored in 1989, and now known as the Don Whillans Memorial Hut, the bothy can be booked through the British Mountaineering Council by small groups of climbers.

WHILE YOU'RE THERE Leek is a magnet for antiques hunters. As well as having a host of antiques dealers, there's an open-air craft and antiques market each Saturday in the historic Market Square. Other markets include the Butter Market, selling mainly fresh traditional produce, on Wednesday, Friday and Saturday.

Hanging Stone and Danebridge

DISTANCE 9.25 miles (14.9km)   **MINIMUM TIME** 5hrs 30min

ASCENT/GRADIENT 1,247ft (380m) ▲▲▲   **LEVEL OF DIFFICULTY** +++

SEE MAP AND INFORMATION PANEL FOR WALK 3

Leaving Walk 3 at Point **Ⓐ**, turn left, signposted 'Swythamley'. Go through the gate, and after 50yds (46m) cross a stile up over a dry-stone wall to the right, following the concessionary path to Hanging Stone. Cross the meadow along the faint path to the next stile, after which the path becomes more obvious. At Hanging Stone, go right down steep steps to the first of two inscriptions that reads:

'Beneath this rock, August 1st 1874 was buried Burke, a noble mastiff black and tan, faithful as woman, braver than man, a gun and a ramble, his heart's desire, with the friend of his life, this Swythamley squire'

Follow the track down to the bottom and turn right, along the wide track to Hangingstone Farm. Just above the farm, the track continues straight on, but the path off to the left should be taken down the hill, to the woods at the bottom. Keep to the left where a concessionary path goes straight on, then descend across a field and driveway to Danebridge.

At the road, descend right to the bridge, take the path to the right and go over a stile just before the bridge at Point **Ⓑ**. Follow the River Dane upstream into woods before going through a gate into a meadow.

Continue along the obvious path before bearing right, up a short rise, to a gate in a fence. Follow the fence left, along a narrow dirt track. Go through two vertical stone posts and come to another stile, followed by two more stone pillars. At Back Dane farmhouse, where the gravel track turns back on itself, continue ahead. Cross the open slope through a wall and, after 200yds (183m), cross a couple of stiles through a wall, then a fence.

Soon after, pass to the right of a farm building, continuing between two fences and then across another stile towards the river. Just after a path comes in from the right you reach a major path junction under a big tree. Go right up the short, sharp slope following signs to Swythamley, and then right again up an easier incline for 0.5 miles (800m). At a rocky outcrop (admire the views from the tops of the rocks) follow signs to Lud's Church, and rejoin Walk 3 at Point **Ⓒ**.

Overleaf: View of the Roaches, a gritstone escarpment (Walk 3)

Rudyard Reservoir

DISTANCE 4.5 miles (7.2km)	**MINIMUM TIME** 1hr 45min	

ASCENT/GRADIENT 180ft (55m) ▲▲▲   **LEVEL OF DIFFICULTY** ✦✦✦

PATHS Gravel bridleways, footpaths and roads

LANDSCAPE Lakeside and woodland

SUGGESTED MAP OS Explorer 268 Wilmslow

START/FINISH Grid reference: SJ939611

DOG FRIENDLINESS Good, but care should be taken near wildfowl

PARKING Car park at northeast corner of reservoir

PUBLIC TOILETS Opposite visitor centre at reservoir's southwest corner

Rudyard Reservoir was built in 1800 to provide an adequate water supply to the region's canals. It wasn't until the second half of the century, however, that it was commercially exploited as a major tourist attraction, thanks to the fast-growing popularity of boating and picnicking among the Victorian middle classes.

ENTERTAINMENT ON THE WATERFRONT

In its heyday, the waterfront would have been awash with holiday-makers escaping from the smoggy industrial towns at weekends, with a funfair, bandstand and dance floor for the adults, and carousels, slides and swings for the children. Ice skating was very popular in the winter, when fairy lights were hung from trees, and great fires on the shore enabled night skating and dancing. The reservoir was also the scene of some amazing spectacles. In June 1861, the memorably named African Blondin walked over the reservoir on a tightrope. (He was a pupil of the great Charles Blondin, renowned for crossing Niagara Falls on a tightrope.) And in June 1877 a poster records that a Captain Webb gave a 'representation in miniature of his cross-Channel feat', after he became the first person to swim from England to France two years earlier.

KIPLING CONNECTION

However, it was at a Victorian picnic in April 1863 that the reservoir's name was assured its place in literary history, when renowned pottery designer John Lockwood Kipling met his bride-to-be Alice Macdonald. History has it that the courting couple spent much of their time here and were so fond of the memories that they named their first son after the reservoir. Rudyard Kipling was born in Bombay on 30 December, 1865 and spent his first five years in India, before being sent to England to stay with a foster family. After finishing his schooling he returned to India to work as a journalist on the *Civil and Military Gazette*, but during his spare time he wrote the first of the poems and stories that later made him famous. He went on to write many more, including his most famous poem, *If*. Despite his popular and critical success, Kipling declined many of the honours that were offered to him, including a knighthood, Poet Laureateship and Order of Merit, but in 1907, aged 42, he accepted the Nobel Prize for Literature.

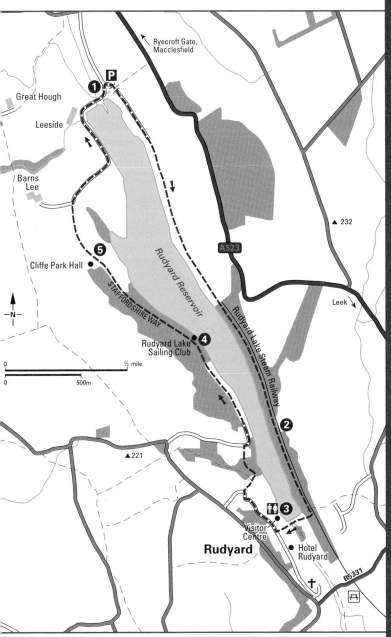

1 From the car park, at the far end of a potholed dirt track off Beat Lane, take the left fork underneath the obvious bridge. Follow the wide, gravel bridleway along the shore, with a mini-gauge railway just to the left (see While You're There). Continue towards the end of the reservoir.

2 Nearing the end and just after the Lakeside Loop signal box there's a short track to the right of the main path up to a scenic picnic area. After this cross the dam at the head of the reservoir (a pay telescope gives wider views).

3 From the visitor centre and toilet block head away from the reservoir up the footpath beside some prominent black railings (not the vehicle drive through the wide gate). At the top is a metalled road. Turn left to reach the Hotel Rudyard, otherwise turn right and then fork left at The Crescent, after which the road becomes a gravel track. Where the track veers right, take the narrow footpath straight ahead (avoiding the private road into the caravan park). Just after the brow of the rise is a junction of two paths. Fork right, then go straight ahead along the road. Go downhill and left on a path before a private drive. At the far end turn right onto a road. Continue above the shore until it becomes unsurfaced at Rudyard Lake Sailing Club.

4 After 400yds (366m) along the wooded path, cross the stile into a clearing with views over the water. The path eases gently uphill to a gate with a chain, which signals your arrival at the vast Victorian pile of Cliffe Park Hall.

5 Continue past the building and down the gently sloping drive. At the far end turn right onto a small, surfaced road, back towards the reservoir. Go over the stile beside the cattle grid and continue around the end of the reservoir to the car park.

WHERE TO EAT AND DRINK From Easter to the end of September, the cafe opposite the visitor centre offers snacks and light refreshments, including hot and cold drinks. For those after something more substantial, the bar at the Hotel Rudyard offers a selection of main meals and bar snacks, Tuesday to Sunday evenings, as well as a Sunday lunchtime carvery.

WHAT TO SEE The visitor centre, in an old boathouse, is home to migrating swallows, which build their nests in the roof space above the water. In 2000 it was feared that building work would scare the birds off permanently, but they returned the following year to produce two broods of chicks.

WHILE YOU'RE THERE At weekends during the summer, you can hire rowing boats. Alternatively, the Rudyard Lake Steam Railway offers a 3-mile (4.8km) round trip along the side of the reservoir on a mini-gauge railway about half the size of a standard narrow-gauge railway. Steam-hauled trains operate at various weekends throughout the year, including bank holiday weekends, and on most weekdays during school holidays. See www.rlsr.org for details.

Mow Cop Castle

DISTANCE 6.25 miles (10.1km)	**MINIMUM TIME** 2hrs 30min	

ASCENT/GRADIENT 660ft (201m) ▲▲▲   **LEVEL OF DIFFICULTY** +++

PATHS Gravel bridleways, footpaths and roads, many stiles

LANDSCAPE Escarpment top, farmland, canal and woodland

SUGGESTED MAP OS Explorer 268 Wilmslow

START/FINISH Grid reference: SJ856573

DOG FRIENDLINESS Should be kept on lead in fields

PARKING Pay car park at Mow Cop Castle (closed at dusk)

PUBLIC TOILETS None on route

The tiny village of Mow Cop and the escarpment on which it is perched has a rich and fascinating history that goes back thousands of years. Its prominent position, visible from five counties, made it the perfect spot for a beacon. It's thought that the Romans may have had a watchtower here; it's known they built a road from nearby Astbury to Biddulph, passing over Nick i' th' Hill, which would have brought them very close to Mow Cop. There's also an abundance of coal, millstone grit and limestone in the region, all of which the Romans would have used.

A CHAIN OF BEACONS

During the reign of Elizabeth I, beacons were lit throughout the country warning of imminent invasion by the Spanish Armada, and there is little doubt that Mow Cop would have been part of this chain. More recently it has been used as a beacon site for special royal events. On 29 July, 1981, by order of Buckingham Palace, a chain of beacons was lit to commemorate the wedding of Prince Charles to Diana Spencer. Prince Charles lit the first beacon at Hyde Park before the message was relayed up and down England. A flare from the Wrekin in Shropshire was meant to signal the lighting of Mow Cop beacon, but because of fog the message was relayed by radio.

AN 18TH-CENTURY FOLLY

Given the village's lofty position, it perhaps comes as no surprise to learn that Mow Cop is famed for its castle which, situated as it is on the massive stone outcrop right at the top of the escarpment, is visible for literally miles around. But this is no ordinary castle and it certainly wasn't built for defensive purposes. In fact it is not a real castle at all, but an elaborate folly made to look like a ruined medieval fortress, as was fashionable at the time. It was built in 1746 by Randle Wilbraham I of Rode Hall as a summer house and as a means of enhancing the view from Rode Hall some 2 miles (3.2km) to the west.

FOR EVERYONE TO SHARE

The castle's tower and wall (the latter little more than a facade) still present a striking silhouette to the east as well as the west, and would certainly have impressed, or riled, rival landowners on both sides of the border. A century or so after it was built, the owner of nearby Keele Hall claimed that part of the summer house was on his land and that part ownership should fall to him. It was eventually ruled that both parties should share the building, but that the public should have free access. The castle and its surrounds were threatened by quarrying in the 1920s and 1930s, but in 1937, after a legal wrangle, the deeds were donated to the National Trust.

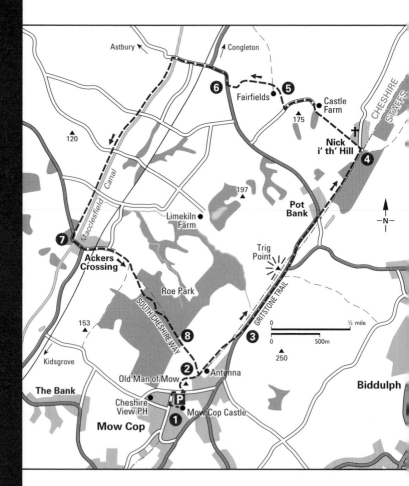

❶ From the castle, turn right along the High Street, then right again up Wood Street. Before you reach the brow of the hill, turn left on the Gritstone Trail to the great rock known as the Old Man of Mow, which is situated on the site of a cairn.

2 Continue along the track to a junction of three paths. Keep ahead, signposted the Gritstone Trail, just to the left of the antenna. Go down steps, and at the end of the narrow field take the upper path (not the more obvious lower track) through woodland.

3 Go left on the metalled road and walk this along the ridge for 0.75 miles (1.2km) until it bends left at Pot Bank Farm. Go straight ahead on the obvious path.

4 Follow this path until it reaches another road. Turn left down the hill and continue straight down another track, to the left of the Methodist church. Just after a house on the right, the path squeezes through a slot in the wall. Stay straight down through the fields, over the stile. At Castle Farm, go through the gate and follow the road round. After 250yds (229m), after a brick shed on your right, go through a gap in the hedge.

5 Keeping to the right of Fairfields, cross the stile under a tree and head left across the field to cross a farm driveway. Keeping the same direction, cross fields and stiles, aiming to the left of the white house in the distance ahead. In the last field, follow the hedge around to the left before crossing another stile onto the road.

6 Head right along this road, going left on Dodds Lane to cross the railway and then the canal. Drop down to the tow path on the Macclesfield Canal and turn right along it for 1.25 miles (2km).

7 At Bridge No. 85 cross the canal and, after 200yds (183m), go left up Yew Tree Lane. Go under the railway, keep right at a wide fork, and after 300yds (274m) take a left fork up a steep track and, soon after, the less obvious gated track, right, into a field. Head right of the farm and follow the hedge up. At the top, cross a stile into the wood.

8 At the top of the wood, cross another stile into a field and continue to the top of the ridge. Turn right and make your way back past the Old Man and into Mow Cop.

WHERE TO EAT AND DRINK The Cheshire View is over 200 years old and, like many of the buildings in Mow Cop, is constructed of local stone. It serves an excellent pint of Marston's, plus a range of main meals and bar snacks on Saturdays and Sundays only (lunchtimes and evenings). On a clear day the view includes the mountains of Wales.

WHAT TO SEE The Old Man of Mow, 65ft (20m) high and 1,100ft (335m) above sea level, is situated on the site of a cairn that is thought to have been an ancient burial mound, although it may also have served as a simple boundary marker separating Cheshire and Staffordshire. The cairn has been reduced to its present slimline status by years of quarrying, although quite why this single column was left is unknown. It may have been used to raise large slabs of gritstone, or as a reminder of the original cairn.

WHILE YOU'RE THERE Little Moreton Hall is an eye-catching, half-timbered Tudor house surrounded by a moat, built in the 1500s for the prosperous Cheshire landowner William Moreton. Its irregular, top-heavy design has seen it likened to a gingerbread house. Now owned by the National Trust, the hall is visible from the walk at the top of the escarpment.

Overleaf: Mow Cop, a hilltop folly owned by the National Trust (Walk 6)

Around Tittesworth Reservoir

DISTANCE 4.5 miles (7.2km)	**MINIMUM TIME** 2hrs 30min

ASCENT/GRADIENT 131ft (40m) ▲▲▲   **LEVEL OF DIFFICULTY** ✦✦✦

PATHS Good, well-made footpaths, forest tracks and roads

LANDSCAPE Reservoir and woodland

SUGGESTED MAP AA Leisure Map 7 Central Peak District

START/FINISH Grid reference: SJ993601

DOG FRIENDLINESS On lead around visitor centre, under control elsewhere

PARKING Reservoir visitor centre (pay car park)

PUBLIC TOILETS At reservoir visitor centre

Tittesworth Reservoir and dam were built in 1858 to collect water from the River Churnet for the benefit of Leek's thriving textile and cloth-dying industry. By 1963 work to increase its size had been completed, and local farmland was flooded to create a reservoir capable of supplying drinking water to Stoke-on-Trent and surrounding areas. With a capacity of 6.5 billion gallons (29.5 billion litres), when full it can supply 10 million gallons (45 million litres) of water every day.

HABITAT FOR WILDLIFE

The land around the reservoir provides a habitat for a wide variety of wildlife, and many creatures can be seen in the course of this walk. Look out for brown hares in the fields near the car park. You can tell them from rabbits by their very long legs, black-tipped ears and a triangular black and light brown tail. Otters were once hunted almost to extinction by dogs, and although the sport is now illegal their numbers remain low. They are nocturnal creatures and not often seen, but look out for their droppings by the water's edge and the tell-tale prints of their webbed feet and wavy line tail prints in the sand and soft mud. Look also for holes in the banks along the River Churnet, where it enters the reservoir. Although it's a difficult little creature to spot, a hole may just be the entrance to a vole burrow and home to a water vole like Ratty from *The Wind in the Willows*.

BATS AND BIRDS

Europe's smallest bat, the pipistrelle, suffered a severe decline in numbers in the last decades of the 20th century due to loss of hunting habitats like hedges, ponds and grassland. Pond restoration near Churnet Bay is encouraging their return and they can best be seen here near dusk, flying at an incredible speed, twisting and turning as they dive to gobble caddisflies, moths and gnats.

Birdlife around the reservoir is abundant and there are two bird hides. Look out particularly for skylarks, small birds with a high-pitched continuous warble, that nest in the meadows around Tittesworth. The song thrush also finds a home here, as does the linnet. Look for the male of the species in spring and summer when it has a bright blood-red breast and forehead. You'll find them in the trees and bushes near the visitor centre and at the hide near the conservation pool.

At various times of the year you might spot barnacle geese, great crested grebes, pied flycatchers, spectacular kingfishers, cormorants and even a rare osprey that has visited several times in recent years.

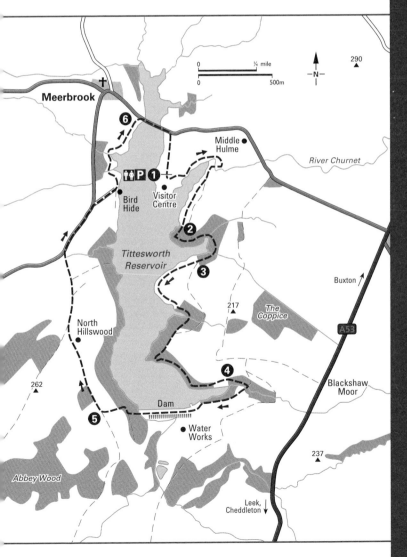

1 Facing the entrance to the visitor centre turn left, cross the car park and follow the path signed 'Waymarked Walk' past the play area. Continue along the hard path as it snakes round the end of the reservoir and crosses two bridges, then go right at a signpost for 'Water's edge path'. At the very far end turn right to rejoin the main track signed 'Long Trail'.

2 Follow the Long Trail through the wood, crossing two small bridges. As the path leaves the wood fork right onto a grassy track, again signed 'Water's edge path'.

3 Continue along the bank of the reservoir, then re-enter woodland and cross some duckboards. Cross a bridge by a picnic table, ascend some steps and turn right to rejoin the wide main track once more. Skirt the edge of a wood, keeping the fence on your left, then go downhill through a wood and along the reservoir bank.

4 Go through some more woodland, cross a bridge, walk up some steps, then continue on a gravel path signposted, at a junction, 'Long Trail to Dam Wall'. Follow the path downhill towards the dam. Go through a gate and cross the dam head. At the far end, go uphill on a series of steps and turn right onto a footpath.

5 Go through a gate and turn right at a T-junction onto a metalled lane. Continue on this through a farm, following the signs for Meerbrook, straight ahead. At the road junction turn right at the Long Trail and Visitor Centre sign. Turn right again, following the road to Tittesworth Reservoir. When this turns to the right, bear left on a footpath beside the reservoir.

6 Go through a gate onto the road, then turn right into the public entrance to the reservoir to return to the visitor centre.

WHERE TO EAT AND DRINK Stop at the Tittesworth Visitor Centre, which is at the start of the walk. This light and airy restaurant has great views over the water and a good selection of food options, ranging from a full breakfast through tasty soups and rolls to afternoon teas with delicious scones and pastries.

WHAT TO SEE Towards the end of the walk look out for Butterfly Beach, an experimental area designed to encourage breeding butterflies. This 'luxury hotel' for these delightful insects has a sandy beach for a spot of sunbathing on a warm summer day, and thistles, nettles and a host of wild flowers to provide egg-laying sites and food.

WHILE YOU'RE THERE A visit to the Churnet Valley Railway will invoke memories of steam travel on a rural railway of the mid-20th century. Starting from the Victorian station at Cheddleton, it meanders along beside the River Churnet and the Cauldon Canal. There are several stops, including the picturesque hamlet of Consall with some fine local walks and The Black Lion public house (see Walk 20).

Along the Manifold Way

DISTANCE 5.5 miles (8.8km)	MINIMUM TIME 3hrs 30min

ASCENT/GRADIENT 518ft (158m) ▲▲▲   LEVEL OF DIFFICULTY ✦✦✦

PATHS Hard surface on Manifold Way, other footpaths can be muddy in wet weather, many stiles

LANDSCAPE Woodland, meadows and valleys

SUGGESTED MAP AA Walker's Map 1 Central Peak District

START/FINISH Grid reference: SK095561

DOG FRIENDLINESS Keep on lead near livestock

PARKING On Manifold Way near Wetton Mill

PUBLIC TOILETS Next to Wetton Mill Tea Room

Described by one local as 'A line starting nowhere and ending up at the same place', the narrow-gauge Leek and Manifold Valley Light Railway was one of England's most picturesque white elephants. Though it survived a mere 30 years from its first run in June 1904, its legacy is still enjoyed today. It ran for 8 miles (12.9km) from Hulme End to Waterhouses, where passengers and freight had to transfer to the standard-gauge Leek branch of the North Staffordshire Railway.

THE LEEK AND MANIFOLD VALLEY LIGHT RAILWAY
The narrow-gauge railway owed its existence to Leek businessmen who feared that their town would lose out because of the newly opened Buxton-to-Ashbourne line. Their solution was to provide a local rail link to the southeast of the county. For the entire period of its existence the railway was a financial disaster, and should probably never have been built. It was only made possible because the Light Railways Act of 1896 provided grants for small projects like this and reduced bureaucracy. Engineer Everard Calthorp, who built the Barsi Railway near Bombay, used the same techniques and design of locomotive for the Leek and Manifold Valley Light Railway as he used in India, and as a result it looked more like a miniature Indian railway than a classic English line.

MILK TRAIN
The potential success of the line was based on the supposition that the Ecton Copper Mines would re-open and that an extension to Buxton would tap into a lucrative tourist market. But the mines didn't re-open and the extension wasn't built. To survive, the railway made a daily collection of milk from farms along the line and hauled produce from the creamery at Ecton for onward transportation to London.

Passenger traffic was light, though tourists did flock to the area on summer weekends and bank holidays for scenic areas like Thor's Cave and Beeston Tor. Even with this seasonal upturn the line never made a profit, and when the creamery shut in 1933 it was the end of the road for the miniature trains. The track was lifted and the bed presented by the railway company to Staffordshire County Council. They had the remarkable foresight and imagination to be one of the first local authorities to take a disused railway line and convert it to a pedestrian path. Today, as the Manifold Way, it is a favourite of walkers and cyclists.

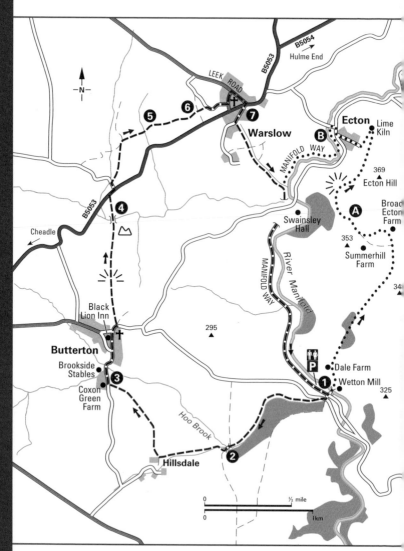

1 At the road junction near the car park, take the lane signposted 'Butterton' opposite the bridge. Just after the road bends sharply right near the ford, go through a gate on the left and walk along a valley-bottom track, with the brook on your left.

2 Cross the footbridge and turn right, signposted 'Hillsdale'. Cross back over the stream and continue on the path as it flanks the hill and then climbs to a farm. At Hillsdale steading turn right, following the footpath over several fields and stiles, heading for the spire at Butterton. Emerge onto the road at Coxon Green Farm.

3 Turn right along the road, cross the ford and then head uphill, forking right to go past the church and the Black Lion Inn. Turn right at a T-junction, go left at a white flagpole, cross two stiles, then head along a spur, through some trees and down a steep hill to cross the stream by a wooden bridge.

4 Head uphill, keeping the hedge on your left, cross two stiles and turn right onto the road. Turn left towards Elkstone, then right across a stile onto the footpath. Cross two stiles, turn

right behind a small derelict building and follow the line of the wall. Cross a stile, then a stream and head uphill, keeping the fence on your left.

5 At the top of the field, just before the fence meets the wall at a large tree, cross a stile on the right. Veer left across the next field, cross another stile, go through a gap in the next fence, then through a gate by a circular water tank. Continue across boggy ground to a junction of paths in the corner of the field where the wall meets the hedge.

6 Go through a gate and ahead through the next field to emerge on the road by Shorecroft Barn. Turn right, then at the end, opposite the church, go left. When you reach the T-junction, turn right onto Leek Road.

7 Turn right again at the next junction, cross the road, then walk down School Lane. Turn left through a gap stile onto a public footpath. Clamber through three more gap stiles, following the course of a stream. Enter a wooded area, go downhill, cross a stile, then turn right to join the Manifold Way. Follow this easy, well-defined trail through an old railway tunnel, back to the car park.

WHERE TO EAT AND DRINK The Black Lion Inn in Butterton is an ideal place to relax in. Children, dogs and walkers are especially welcome and there is a wide range of food available, including a selection for vegetarians. Real ales on tap include Morland Old Speckled Hen and Theakston Black Bull Bitter.

WHAT TO SEE The walk passes through a tunnel that served the old railway. This is close to Swainsley Hall, the home of the Wardle family at the time of construction. They were shareholders in the company building the railway line, and although happy to take any profits going, they did not want to see the trains from their house.

WHILE YOU'RE THERE Visit the old station at Hulme End. Now the Manifold Valley Visitor Centre, it has excellent displays on the history of the Leek and Manifold Valley Light Railway and the industries and communities it served. There are also several relics from the days of steam, and a scale model of the line with Hulme End Station as it was in its heyday.

Overleaf: The Manifold Valley (Walk 8)

Ecton Hill

DISTANCE 4 miles (6.4km)   **MINIMUM TIME** 2hrs

ASCENT/GRADIENT 900ft (274m) ▲▲▲   **LEVEL OF DIFFICULTY** +++

SEE MAP AND INFORMATION PANEL FOR WALK 8

From the car park, Point ❶, cross the bridge over the river and bear left up a wide gravel track. Proceed through Dale Farm and over the stile, continuing up the middle of the gently sloping valley. When the path reaches the woods, veer left as the ground steepens significantly. Cross the stile after the woods, before making a dog-leg right then left, through a narrow slot in the dry-stone wall. Carry on up this shallow valley, heading right along the faint trail to the gap between the trees.

After the gap, head for the corner of a dry-stone wall and continue up the path. At the second gate turn left along the rough road. Just before the farm straight ahead, follow the signs to Summerhill and Lime Kiln. Cross over the stone stile, following the track. At the top left corner of this field, go through the gate and continue straight up the slope, keeping close to the dry-stone wall to your right. Head for the gate at the obvious corner of two walls, Point ❹.

Go through the gate and half left across the field in the direction of the wall, and go down the other side of the hill. Go through the gate and drop down 30 paces until you reach a path skirting right around the hill. Follow this path until it rounds an obvious corner. Follow the path to the top of a scree slope surrounded by a small horseshoe of trees.

Above the scree, just to the right of the track, is a well-preserved mineshaft entrance with a red metal gate set into the exposed rock. A small, lone tree provides an ideal spot for a rest before continuing to the conical stone building (Lime Kiln) straight ahead. From the kiln, walk down the steep, grassy slope (take care here, boots or trainers with good grip are recommended) keeping the dry-stone wall to your right. At the bottom of this clearing are a stone stile and some steps leading to the courtyard of an impressive and rambling old building. Follow the track down to the road, then head right, then left to join the Manifold Way, Point ❸. Follow this to join Walk 8 shortly before the tunnel and take the route back to the car park.

The Market Town of Leek

DISTANCE 4.25 miles (6.8km)	MINIMUM TIME 1hr 45min
ASCENT/GRADIENT 420ft (128m) ▲▲▲	LEVEL OF DIFFICULTY ✦✦✦
PATHS Meadow track and some road walking, many stiles	
LANDSCAPE Hillside meadow and woodland	
SUGGESTED MAP AA Leisure Map 7 Central Peak District	
START/FINISH Grid reference: SJ977569	
DOG FRIENDLINESS Must be kept on lead at all times	
PARKING Roadside parking on Abbey Green Road	
PUBLIC TOILETS None on route (nearest in Leek town centre)	

Leek is an ancient market town that has long been associated with the textile industry. These days, the silks for which it was once renowned have largely been replaced by synthetic alternatives, although a number of textile manufacturers and factory shops selling brand names direct to the public still remain. But it's a little corn mill on the outskirts of the town, built by an illiterate millwright, that put Leek right at the forefront of the Industrial Revolution.

BRINDLEY'S BRILLIANCE

James Brindley was born at Tunstead, near Buxton in Derbyshire, in 1716, and in 1726 his family moved to Leek. He was apprenticed to millwright Abraham Bennett, and after nine years he set up on his own as a millwright in Leek. It was here that he designed and built the water-powered corn mill that today houses a museum to his life and work. However, it wasn't as a millwright that Brindley made his name, but as a designer and builder of canals. In 1759 the Duke of Bridgewater hired him to devise a system to transport coal cheaply from Worsley to Manchester. Brindley's solution was a 10-mile (16.1km) canal that included an underground channel and an aqueduct.

THE CANAL AGE

The scale and complexity of the project was unprecedented, and when the Bridgewater Canal was completed in 1765, it revolutionised the way goods were transported in the north of England. Brindley engineered the Trent and Mersey Canal, the Staffordshire and Worcestershire Canal and many others. In total, he was responsible for 360 miles (579km) of canals, which had a huge impact on both the local and national economies. He undertook all of his engineering feats without any written calculations or drawings, preferring instead to do everything in his head.

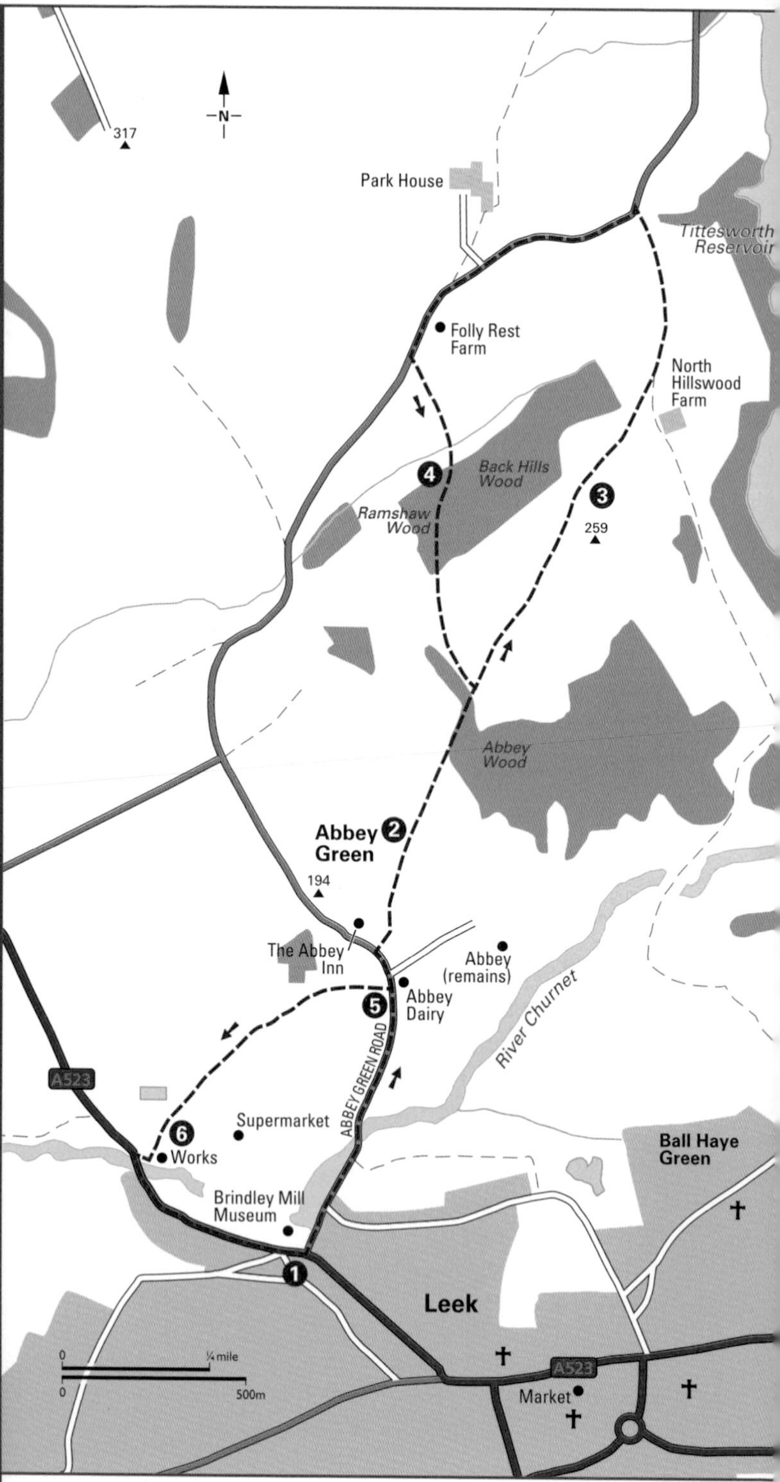

▲ 317

—N—

Park House

Tittesworth
Reservoir

● Folly Rest
Farm

North
Hillswood
Farm

4

*Back Hills
Wood*

*Ramshaw
Wood*

3

259 ▲

*Abbey
Wood*

**Abbey
Green** **2**

194 ▲
●

The Abbey ●
Inn

Abbey ●
(remains)

5
● Abbey
Dairy

River Churnet

A523

ABBEY GREEN ROAD

● Supermarket

**Ball Haye
Green**

✝

6
● Works

● Brindley Mill
Museum

1

Leek

0 | ¼ mile
0 | 500m

✝

A523

Market ●

✝

✝

1 From the museum turn left along the A523, and immediately left again along Abbey Green Road. Follow this, bearing left over a bridge, to Abbey Green. At The Abbey Inn, turn right through the car park and go up the obvious path. After 30 paces, cross a stile and walk diagonally left to the top of the slope.

2 At the top bear right, keeping the fence close to your left. Proceed through a gate into Abbey Wood where the path becomes wider. After a kissing gate carry on up the bridleway until it becomes a grassy track. Aim just to the left of a small copse on the very top of the hill ahead. Continue to a slot in the wall at the corner of Back Hills Wood.

3 Follow the faint track, keeping the dry-stone wall just to your right. At the bottom of the hill go through a gate and join a farm track, keeping North Hillswood Farm to your right. Turn left onto a rough surfaced lane until you reach a metalled road at the end. Turn left and 100yds (91m) after Folly Rest, cross a stile on the left.

Descend, keeping the hedge to your left, and via a gate follow the track to the wood.

4 Go over the stile and pick your way along the narrow path through the holly of Ramshaw Wood. At the top right-hand corner, cross the stile and keep going straight, keeping the bank of trees to your right. At the end of these trees go ahead along the bridleway and retrace your steps back to Abbey Green.

5 Opposite Abbey Dairy go right, over a stile, for a waymarked field path and continue in the same direction over a succession of small aluminium gates. After the fifth continue along the field-edge, with the fence on your left. At the far top left corner of the next field, cross a stile to the left and descend, now with the hedge and fence to your right.

6 At the bottom, cross the stile and head right past the house. At a metalled road, go left, and then left again along the A523, back to Brindley Mill.

WHERE TO EAT AND DRINK The Abbey Inn has a splendid stone patio, overlooking Abbey Green and the Churnet Valley, and a warm, cosy interior. Bar snacks and meals are served every lunchtime and evening (closed all day Monday and Tuesday).

WHAT TO SEE Brindley Mill is a water-powered corn mill with a riverside garden. It illustrates James Brindley's talents as an architect and a millwright and has a small museum dedicated to his life. It's open weekends from Easter to the end of September 2–5pm, and some weekdays in July and August.

WHILE YOU'RE THERE Make sure you take a little time to visit St Edward's Church. It boasts a fine 13th-century roof in which every beam has been hewn from a separate oak tree. Leek's market is held every Wednesday in the Market Place, while the Butter Market is open Friday and Saturday.

Endon's Springs

DISTANCE 3.5 miles (5.7km)	**MINIMUM TIME** 1hr 30min

ASCENT/GRADIENT 269ft (82m) ▲▲▲   **LEVEL OF DIFFICULTY** ✦✦✦

PATHS Easy meadow paths and some roads, many stiles

LANDSCAPE Hillside meadow, forest and farmland

SUGGESTED MAP OS Explorer 258 Stoke-on-Trent

START/FINISH Grid reference: SJ928537

DOG FRIENDLINESS Must be kept on lead at all times

PARKING St Luke's Church car park (Saturdays only), otherwise roadside

PUBLIC TOILETS None on route

The name Endon means 'place where lambs are reared', but today the village is best known, not for its mutton, but for its water. The area around Endon, and in fact most of Derbyshire and northern Staffordshire, features an abundance of natural springs. These springs owe their existence to the local geology. The primarily limestone landscape of the Staffordshire moorlands and the rest of the Peak District is intermittently overlaid by a layer of gritstone. As the latter is a non-porous rock, when the water table rises higher than the limestone, water is forced out at the points on the surface where the two rock layers meet. This constant supply of fresh water was doubtless what prompted ancient peoples to settle in the area.

THE BLACK DEATH

These early settlers began blessing this water supply by adorning local wells with flowers, a ritual known today as well dressing. Its origins are shrouded in mystery: many sources attribute the practice to the period of the Black Death (1348–49) when it's thought that a third of the country's population died of the virus. Some villages remained untouched and, probably quite rightly, attributed this to the clean water supply drawn from their wells. However, it's possible that the custom goes back further, perhaps to Celtic times, and the fact that many well dressings have a 'well queen' suggests echoes of ancient fertility rites and rituals.

WELL DRESSING

Today, well dressing is an annual tradition unique to the central and southern Peak, with a succession of villages dressing their wells between the end of May and early September. Endon's ceremony, which was revived in 1845, traditionally takes place on the Spring Bank Holiday, when two wells are dressed in an elaborate ceremony.

INTRICATE PICTURES

The well dressing itself is usually as intricate as it is elaborate. It is achieved by making a picture, often of a religious theme, out of flowers and petals. The picture is created within a wooden frame filled with soft, wet clay. An outline of the drawing is made using bark, twigs and berries before the spaces are filled in with coloured petals. The picture is made from the bottom upwards so that the petals overlap and rainwater drains off. The finished image is often so ornate it really has to be seen to be believed. Because of the nature of the materials, dressings have to be made in the two or three days just before the ceremony, and they usually only last a week or so. In addition, a well dressing queen is crowned and, on the Bank Holiday Monday, a fair is held in the village, complete with parade, morris dancing and a tossing the sheaf competition.

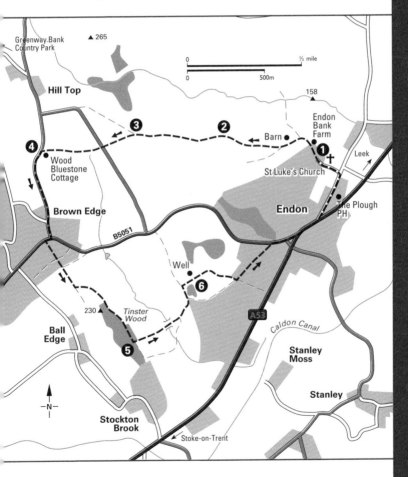

1 From St Luke's Church follow the lane uphill. At the top go right, through the gate for Endon Bank Farm, and after a second gate join a wide track ahead/left. Follow the track round to the left and, 50yds (46m) after a barn on the right, go through a slot in the wall. Cut off the corner of the field to reach a stile, and maintain this direction to reach a double stile on the far side.

2 Continue in the same direction, keeping a hedge just to your left. Cross the stile at the far side of the field and proceed to another old stile straight ahead. Keep straight on uphill until you reach a well-hidden slot in the top left corner of the wall. Continue up the slope, this time with the hedge to your right.

3 At the top right corner of this field, go straight across the stile and continue along the rough track to a road. Go straight over and across three stiles, following a hedge on the left. Cross yet more stiles, aiming for the far left corner of the field by Wood Bluestone Cottage.

4 Turn left down the road and, at the junction with the B5051, go right, then first left along a signed footpath,

over a residential road and up a wide, fenced track. Stay on this as it curves left to the top of the hill and then continues down and along the edge of Tinster Wood. As soon as the track enters the wood proper, head sharp left down a narrow path, somewhat indistinct in places, following it to the bottom left-hand corner.

5 Go through a slot in the wall to your left. Continue straight across a field, keeping the wall to your right, through a pair of wall slots. Cross the small footbridge beneath a tree before crossing a field. At a kissing gate go left up a walled track and left along the road. After 100yds (91m) go right, following the footpath sign beside woodland.

6 At the bottom of this field go through a gate to a surfaced road, following it round to the left. When you reach a proper residential road, go hard left along a rougher track to a surfaced road. Head right and, shortly after, turn left along the A53. Just before you get to The Plough on the left, head left up the road signed to St Luke's Church.

WHERE TO EAT AND DRINK The Plough is conveniently located on the A53 right in the middle of Endon. Standard bar snacks and pub food are available seven days a week and a popular carvery is served daily, all year round.

WHAT TO SEE Despite the reverence in which some wells are clearly held, many are seen only as marks on a map, often existing below the surface. When they do spring up, they're often indicated by little more than a tap, or in some cases, an algae-stained bath tub!

WHILE YOU'RE THERE Greenway Bank Country Park, just to the northwest of Endon, features an arboretum, picnic sites and 114 acres (46ha) of secluded forest around Serpentine Pool and Knypersley Reservoir. A weekend visitor centre provides more local information.

Cheddleton Flint Mill and Deep Hayes

DISTANCE 3.25 miles (5.3km)   MINIMUM TIME 1hr 30min

ASCENT/GRADIENT 272ft (83m) ▲▲▲   LEVEL OF DIFFICULTY ✚✚✚

PATHS Tow path, field and woodland paths (can be muddy), many stiles

LANDSCAPE Canal, reservoir, forest and farmland

SUGGESTED MAP AA Leisure Map 7 Central Peak District

START/FINISH Grid reference: SJ961533

DOG FRIENDLINESS On lead in country park, off lead along tow path

PARKING Deep Hayes Country Park visitor centre (closed at dusk)

PUBLIC TOILETS Deep Hayes Country Park visitor centre

The walk starts at Deep Hayes Country Park, a recreational area which has been created around a disused reservoir. The reservoir itself was built in 1849 to compensate the River Churnet for the loss of water to several mills further downstream, while at the same time works were completed at nearby Wall Grange to pump drinking water from Caena's Well. During the 1830s and 1840s thousands died in cholera epidemics because of poor water, so clean water was needed to serve the growing population of the booming Potteries region.

FORMER RESERVOIR

The reservoir at Deep Hayes was formed behind an earth dam 50ft (15m) high and 400ft (122m) long, which was built by hand. It continued to 'top up' the River Churnet until as recently as 1979, when problems with the dam's structure became too costly to repair. The water level was reduced, and three separate pools were made to create the country park you see today, complete with trails, toilets and visitor centre.

THE FLINT MILL

The highlight of the walk, though, is undoubtedly the flint mill on the Caldon Canal. Originally a corn mill dating as far back as the 13th century, it was strengthened for flint grinding in 1800. Flint is a hard, nearly pure form of silica; when ground down to a fine powder it's used to harden and whiten pottery (before flint was used, silica was added in the form of fine sand, but the sand was often iron-stained and impure).

THE PRODUCTION PROCESS

The flint arrived by narrow boat. It was heated in kilns at 2,012°F (1,100°C) to make it more brittle, a process known as 'calcining'. The heated flint was then broken up and ground into fine powder by the water-powered, and later steam-driven, millstones. The slip, a mixture of water and fine flint powder, would be dried into blocks called 'cake' and taken to the wharf for dispatch to the potteries.

GRINDING ON

The mill continued to be worked well into the 20th century. During World War II, George Edwards & Son ground rutile (a black or reddish-brown mineral) for welding rods and, as late as the 1960s, ceramic stains were ground here for potteries overseas (in Saudi Arabia and Finland, for example). The mill finally stopped grinding flint in 1963, but it's open to visitors most weekends and on bank holidays.

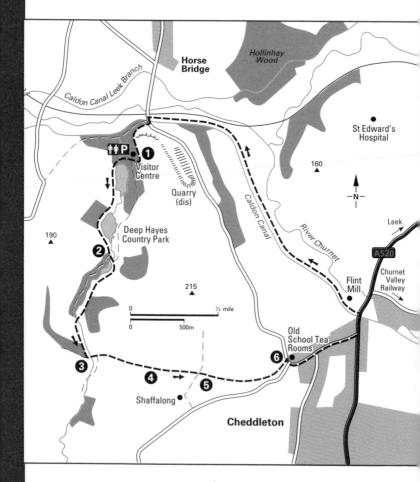

❶ From the visitor centre in Deep Hayes Country Park go down to the bottom of the car park and cross the stream before following the shore of the reservoir along a wooded track. Go up some steps and left before the stile, continuing above the shoreline. After the second reservoir and at a fork of two obvious footpaths, go left down some steep steps and across the concrete stepping stones.

2 Once across the stream head right through a fence gap with a sign that says 'Keep dogs on leads'. Shortly this track runs alongside the small stream that fills the reservoirs. When you cross back over the stream, continue to follow it to the left through an aluminium kissing gate, then up some steps beyond a wooden gate ahead.

3 At a path junction (marked by a wooden signpost) head down steps left, back over the stream, then follow the public footpath sign to Cheddleton. After crossing a stile, go right for 30yds (27m) before continuing up the wooded hill on steps. At the top of the wood cross the stile and head straight across the field, aiming left of the farm.

4 In the far corner of the field go along the muddy farm track to a

gate. From here follow the obvious, waymarked path over a succession of stiles through a series of small fields to the left of the farm buildings.

5 Beyond a double stile and plank footbridge, by a wooden public footpath sign, head straight across the field following the line of trees to your left. After the final tree veer right and cross the small stile over a dry-stone wall and, dropping downhill, cross the next field to its far side. To the left of a clump of trees is a stile, followed quickly by another stile and a slot in the wall, bringing you out onto the road into Cheddleton almost opposite the tea rooms.

6 At the end of this road, head left on the pavement of the A520 and, after 100yds (91m), turn left following signs to the flint mill. Continue along the tow path for a mile (1.6km) until you reach a bridge (No. 39) over the canal. Cross over the bridge, before turning right, along the driveway, to return to the visitor centre.

WHERE TO EAT AND DRINK The Old School Tea Rooms offers a fantastic range of food and drinks, from main meals through to snacks and cakes, home-made soup, freshly made sandwiches and baguettes, as well as an all-day brunch. Try the house speciality, Staffordshire oatcakes with a variety of fillings. There is also a small craft centre here, which sells an amazing array of locally produced gifts, including pottery, paintings, photography and needlework. Open Wednesday–Sunday, 10am–4pm, all year round.

WHAT TO SEE The Caldon Canal, running from Froghall to Etruria Junction on the Trent and Mersey Canal in Stoke-on-Trent, was the brainchild of canal-building genius James Brindley. Flint came from Cheddleton on the Caldon Canal, while high-quality clay came from the West Country, via the Mersey and the Trent and Mersey Canal.

WHILE YOU'RE THERE The Churnet Valley Railway runs from Cheddleton to Froghall and back again on various dates throughout the year (up to five days a week in summer). All trips are steam-powered in restored locomotives, and stop at Consall and Leek in addition to Cheddleton and Froghall. All stations have a nearby tea room or pub for a bite to eat, in addition to other attractions, such as the museum and engine shed at Cheddleton, idyllic canal walking at Consall and the Brindley Mill Museum at Leek (see Walk 10). For a timetable, visit Cheddleton Station or www.churnetvalley-railway.co.uk.

From Grindon to Thor's Cave

DISTANCE 5 miles (8km)	**MINIMUM TIME** 3hrs 30min	

ASCENT/GRADIENT 423ft (129m) ▲▲▲   **LEVEL OF DIFFICULTY** ✦✦✦

PATHS Forest tracks, grass and mud, hard footpath, several stiles

LANDSCAPE Hillside, valley, meadows and woodland

SUGGESTED MAP AA Leisure Map 7 Central Peak District

START/FINISH Grid reference: SK085545

DOG FRIENDLINESS Keep on lead near livestock

PARKING At Grindon church

PUBLIC TOILETS None on route

Anyone who has seen *The Lair of the White Worm* (1988) will recognise at once the entrance to Thor's Cave and may, as a result, feel slightly apprehensive when climbing the path up the hillside. The opening shot in the film features the famous landmark and, as the blood-red titles roll, the camera slowly zooms in towards the mouth of the cave.

SCENE OF A HORROR FILM

Based loosely on Bram Stoker's last novel, *The Lair of the White Worm* stars Amanda Donahoe, Hugh Grant, Catherine Oxenburg, Peter Capaldi and Sammi Davis. Stoker's original story was based in the Peak District in the 19th century and tells of odd disappearances, legends of a fearsome giant serpent and of the strange and sinister Lady Arabella. Film-maker Ken Russell moved the whole story in time to the 20th century and altered the plot considerably.

A young Scottish archaeology student, Angus Flint (Peter Capaldi) finds a mysterious, reptilian skull at an excavation he's working on near his lodgings. Later he takes the two sisters who run the guest house to the home of Lord James D'Ampton (Hugh Grant) for the annual celebrations to commemorate the slaying of the D'Ampton Worm by his ancestor. Angus leaves early to escort one of the sisters, Mary (Sammi Davis) home. Passing through woods near where her parents mysteriously disappeared they encounter the snakelike Lady Sylvia (Amanda Donahoe). In the dark cellars of her Gothic mansion she has been worshipping an evil and ancient snake god. It has an insatiable appetite for virgin flesh and Mary's sister Eve (Catherine Oxenburg) is on the menu. D'Ampton connects the disappearance of Eve with Lady Sylvia and heads for Thor's Cave to search for a tunnel connecting to Temple Hall. The nonsense ends with Angus emerging as the reluctant hero, snatching Eve from the monster's jaws and slaying it.

Thor's Cave may be the most famous cave in the Peak District, but there are others, including Ossom's Cave and Elderbush. Both have revealed bones and flints from the Stone and Bronze Ages. Thor's Cave may have been home to prehistoric beasties, but in reality none of them were big white snakes. Formed over thousands of years from the effects of wind and rain on the soft limestone, it probably sheltered animals like giant red deer, bears or even early humans. Excavations have revealed it was the site of a Bronze Age burial, but much of the evidence was lost by over-zealous 19th-century excavators.

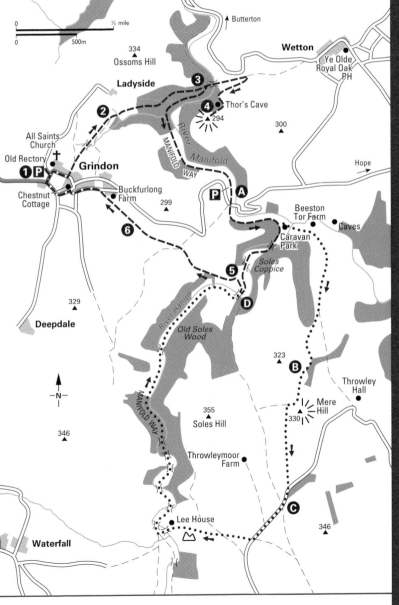

1 From the car park turn left and left again past the play area and head downhill. After 200yds (183m) go left onto a public footpath, go through a gap stile, cross a field and head downhill on the right of two diverging paths. Cross a bridge, go through a gate and head downhill, keeping the stream and the wood on your right.

2 At the wall at the far end go through a gap stile on your right, continuing downhill into National Trust land at Ladyside. Cross over a stile, go through a wood and then leave it via another stile. Turn right, still continuing downhill to reach a stile leading onto the Manifold Way.

3 Cross the Manifold Way, then a bridge and take the path uphill following the signs for Thor's Cave. At the mouth of the cave turn left, continue on a track uphill, curve right before a stile and follow the path to the summit for superb views along the Manifold Valley.

4 Retrace your steps to the Manifold Way and turn left. Continue past a car park, then at the caravan park bear right on the Manifold Way to cross two bridges. At the beginning of the third bridge cross a stile on the right (signposted 'Grindon') and follow the path back, parallel to the road and then curving left and uphill.

5 Go through one gate, then another by a dried-up pond and follow the path uphill, with the wall on your right. Keep straight on, through successive fields, with the church spire at Grindon ahead.

6 Maintain your direction across fields, keeping to the left of the farm. Finally join a farm road, continue along a walled path, then turn right onto the road opposite Chestnut Cottage. Take the first left and follow this road back to the car park.

WHERE TO EAT AND DRINK From the summit slope of Thor's Cave, a footpath runs eastwards across the fields for just under a mile (1.6km) to Wetton. Ye Olde Royal Oak is located in the centre of the village and has long been a popular destination for walkers. The 400-year-old pub offers a choice of decent real ales, as well as hot and cold food served daily. If the weather is fine, you can sit outside in the beer garden and relax.

WHAT TO SEE Near the church gates in Grindon is an old stone known as the Rindle Stone. It contains the inscription 'The lord of the manor of Grindon established his right to this Rindle at Staffordshire Assizes on March 17th 1862'. A rindle is a brook that only flows in wet weather. Why anyone would want to establish legal right to such a thing is not explained on the stone.

WHILE YOU'RE THERE All Saints Church in Grindon is well worth a visit. Known as 'the Cathedral of the Moorlands', it contains the remains of an earlier Saxon church, an ancient font and stone coffins. There's also a memorial to the airmen and journalists who died in a plane crash on Grindon Moor during the terrible winter of 1947 when attempting to bring relief supplies to the village.

Beeston Tor and Mere Hill

DISTANCE 8.5 miles (13.7km)   **MINIMUM TIME** 5hrs

ASCENT/GRADIENT 930ft (283m) ▲▲▲   **LEVEL OF DIFFICULTY** +++

SEE MAP AND INFORMATION PANEL FOR WALK 13

From the car park, Point **Ⓐ**, continue along the Manifold Way until you reach a stile on the left. Cross over to join the parallel track, go through the caravan park and over a bridge, following the wide gravel track round and up the side of a hill, forking right just before Beeston Tor Farm.

After 250yds (229m) of steady climbing, cross over a stile and carry on along a wide track past an abandoned barn on the left. Continue through a gate, following the hollow of the valley up the faint grass tracks to the corner of a dry-stone wall, just before the band of trees on the crest of the slope. (Look back over your shoulder here at the impressive cliffs and caves of Beeston Tor.) At the corner of the wall ignore the footpath sign pointing off to the left, instead continue straight up the slope with the dry-stone wall on your right to reach a prominent band of trees, Point **Ⓑ**.

Shortly after the signpost, cross a stone stile and then another stile at the top of the next field. Carry on over a false horizon and make for the summit of Mere Hill. At the summit head right along the dry-stone wall for about 100yds (91m) and then go left through a breach in the collapsed wall.

Continue straight across the field to a gate and carry on across the next field, aiming for the right-hand end of a copse straight ahead, Point **Ⓒ**. When you reach the road at Point **Ⓒ**, head right for 400yds (366m) until you cross a cattle grid, then cross the stile to the right just past a more obvious gravel track.

From here you can follow a footpath all the way down to the Manifold Way (keep to the right, but it's quite steep and may be muddy after rain, so suitable footwear is essential). At the bottom of the hill, just to the left of Lee House, cross a footbridge to your left to rejoin the Manifold Way. Go right and stay on this path for 1.75 miles (2.8km) until you come to the stile on the left just after a bridge (signposted 'Grindon'), Point **Ⓓ**. Continue on the original route on Walk 13.

Overleaf: Tableware at the Emma Bridgewater Shop on Lichfield Street, Stoke-on-Trent (Walk 15)

Stoke-on-Trent's Potteries

DISTANCE 3 miles (4.8km)	**MINIMUM TIME** 1hr 15min
ASCENT/GRADIENT 262ft (80m) ▲▲▲	**LEVEL OF DIFFICULTY** ✚✚✚

PATHS Pavement and hill trail

LANDSCAPE Streets and urban parkland

SUGGESTED MAP OS Explorer 258 Stoke-on-Trent

START/FINISH Grid reference: SJ874501

DOG FRIENDLINESS Must be on lead near roads; not suitable for factory shop

PARKING Ample parking on Moorland Road by Burslem Park

PUBLIC TOILETS On Market Place in town centre

The City of Stoke-on-Trent, known as 'the Potteries,' actually consists of six towns, each with its own sense of history, character and identity: Burslem, Fenton, Hanley, Longton, Tunstall and Stoke itself. All six owe their existence to the rich seams of coal and clay in the area which originally would have been mined at or near the surface. Both coal and clay were mined by the Romans, and excavations at Trent Vale in the 1950s uncovered a pottery kiln and workshop dating from the first century AD. But it was in Burslem in the 16th century that the pottery revolution got under way, thanks largely to the efforts of one man, Josiah Wedgwood.

FACTORY PRODUCTION TAKES HOLD

In addition to being a talented craftsmen and an astute businessman, Wedgwood was also an innovator – he was the first to establish a factory for making fine pots. Until then pottery had been a cottage industry, but Wedgwood's Burslem factory set a new standard, and before long similar buildings were springing up all over Stoke. Today, Burslem still boasts the highest concentration of potteries in the city, several of them visited on this short walk. The first is Moorland Pottery, based on the historic Chelsea Works site, while a little further on near Market Place is the factory shop for Royal Stafford, whose ceramic tableware is still produced locally.

Despite economic downturns and changing markets, Burslem retains its industrial core and a long-standing reputation as the 'Mother Town' of Stoke-on-Trent. This is an urban landscape of period factories, small warehouses and historic canals, as well as grand municipal buildings, some in better shape than others and many now given over to bars and shops. Although a few of the large ceramic producers have gone, many that remain are small in scale but high in value, producing sought-after tableware and collectables. New business parks have been established around the town's fringes to cater for this growing business.

MIXED FORTUNES

Heading down Nile Street you pass the site of the former Royal Doulton works, where the Staffordshire tradition of china figurines was first established. In 2005 the factory closed when production was switched overseas, and the site is being redeveloped. A little further on is Dudson Factory Outlet, where you can browse a wide range of high-quality but reasonably priced tableware that the firm has been producing for the catering industry for well over a century. Next up is the Moorcroft Factory Shop, while a little further on is their Heritage Visitor Centre, complete with original bottle kiln and open daily, except Sunday. Moorcroft has been making fine china for over 100 years and each piece is hand-crafted by skilled craftsmen. The guided factory tour allows you to watch the unique processes at first hand, including the application of the design onto the pot which is known as tubelining – they say it's like icing a cake, just a little more difficult.

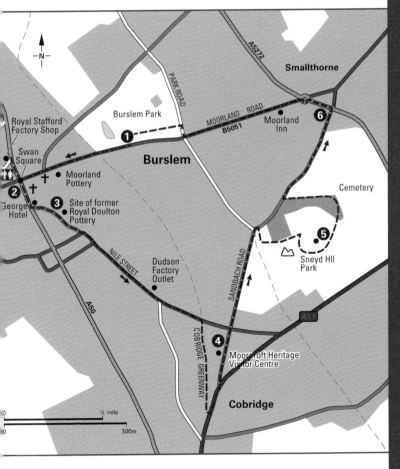

1 From Burslem Park head down Moorland Road past Moorland Pottery into the town centre. At the busy junction at Swan Square turn right and walk uphill for 100 yards (91m) to visit the Royal Stafford factory shop on the left, which includes a small cafe.

2 Retrace your steps to the junction and keep going straight over, downhill past the war memorial on Swan Bank. Take the second left, just past the imposing George Hotel.

3 Walk down Nile Street, past the site of the former Royal Doulton factory on the left. Go past Dudson Factory Outlet and the Moorcroft Factory Shop and continue along the road. Just before the bridge go right onto a ramp up to the leafy Cobridge Greenway cycle trail, a former railway line. Turn right and follow this to the end. Turn left, then quickly left again onto Sandbach Road to reach the Moorcroft Heritage Visitor Centre.

4 After visiting the museum continue along Sandbach Road and keep going over the traffic-lights. After 400yds (366m), just as the road eases round to the right, turn sharp right up the gravel path into Sneyd Hill Park. Immediately take a left fork straight up the hill, following the steep slope to the top for excellent views.

5 From the top of the hill start to walk back down the way you came, but soon bear left on an obvious trail contouring round the hill to the left. Follow this round and down to the bottom, near the cemetery. Turn left and follow the grassy track around the base of the hill until it rejoins the road. Turn right and walk up the broad pavement to the junction at the top of the hill.

6 Turn sharp left, then left again at the final mini-roundabout, past the Moorland Inn and down Moorland Road. After about 500yds (457m) turn right onto Park Road, then immediately left to enter Burslem Park and an excellent spot for a picnic to end the walk.

WHERE TO EAT AND DRINK Although a chain pub, the Moorland Inn offers a varied, good-value menu of traditional pub food mixed with Tex-Mex classics. There are picnic benches at the back and food is served all day long, seven days a week, year-round.

WHAT TO SEE Take time to soak up the views of Burslem and the rest of Stoke from the vantage point at the top of Sneyd Hill. Burslem Park is a green oasis amid the urban bustle and is undergoing a major restoration of its gardens, paths and historic buildings with Lottery funding.

WHILE YOU'RE THERE Ford Green Hall, a mile (1.6km) northeast of Sneyd Hill, is a 17th-century farmhouse with a museum and period Tudor garden. It's been restored and furnished with an outstanding collection of local textiles, ceramics and furniture, while the herb garden shows how plants were once used for medicinal and even cosmetic purposes. Open Sunday to Thursday, 1–5pm, all year.

Apedale Country Park

DISTANCE 4.75 miles (7.7km)	MINIMUM TIME 2hrs

ASCENT/GRADIENT 300ft (91m) ▲▲▲   LEVEL OF DIFFICULTY ✦✦✦

PATHS Wide gravel tracks, roads and dirt trails, many stiles

LANDSCAPE Ancient woodland, farmland and hilltop

SUGGESTED MAP OS Explorer 258 Stoke-on-Trent

START/FINISH Grid reference: SJ823484

DOG FRIENDLINESS Under close control in the country park

PARKING Car park opposite Heritage Centre, gates close at dusk

PUBLIC TOILETS At Heritage Centre

Apedale Community Country Park, west of Newcastle-under-Lyme, has a rich and varied history. Its name has two possible meanings: one suggests that the word ape comes from the Latin *apis* meaning bee; the other is that ape is short for apple. Whichever you prefer, it seems probable that Apedale was once an ancient rural landscape, although for the last 2,000 years, it has been anything but...

IRON AND COAL

Iron smelting in Apedale probably goes back at least to Roman times, if not before. Mining in the area dates back as far as the 1200s. This was made possible thanks to large deposits of coal lying at or very near the surface. Of the four main Staffordshire deposits, the Potteries Coalfield was the biggest, comprising an area of 100 square miles (259sq km). The Potteries, though, were doubly blessed. Not only was there coal to be mined and sold, but there were rich seams of high-quality clays that could be used to make pots. As the pottery industry developed, so the demand for coal increased, and the Apedale collieries would have played a major role in meeting that demand. The arrival of the first canals in 1777, thanks partly to the vision of people like Josiah Wedgwood, precipitated a boom in business throughout the region, and the emergence of the railways 60 years later proved to be another catalyst to productivity and prosperity.

A MAJOR CENTRE OF PRODUCTION

With the Industrial Revolution well under way, iron mining and smelting enjoyed its own boom thanks to the invention of the blast furnace in the late 18th century. Apedale was a major centre of production, at one point employing more than 3,000 men. Rising costs, however, sent local industry into decline by the 1920s, and when the owners lost their fortune in the Wall Street Crash, it ended altogether. Coal mining in the area, however, continued until 1998, when the last deep mine was closed at Silverdale, just a mile or two to the south of Apedale.

RECLAMATION WORK

For much of the 20th century Apedale remained a barren and desolate place, but today little evidence of the area's industrial heritage remains. Nature has reclaimed the spoil heaps with luxurious ferns (see Fern Bank, on the map), and trees are recolonising the land, creating woodland, meadows and pools. Active reclamation work and continued efforts to improve and develop the park and its facilities reflect a triumph of nature over industry. Apedale Community Country Park is probably as green now as it's been in the last 300 years.

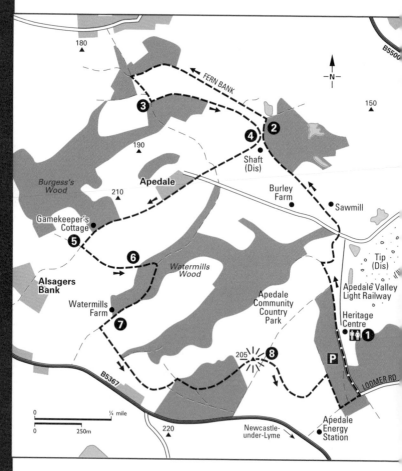

❶ From the Heritage Centre in Apedale Community Country Park take a path to go right, through a gate. After 400yds (366m) turn right down to a corner of the park, then continue straight ahead, passing to the left of the sawmill. At a fork in the path, head right down a short hill to reach the corner of a lake.

2 Ignoring the stile, turn left along the narrow path into the woods. Stay on the main path, cross a plank footbridge, then go right at a fork to emerge into Fern Bank. Follow this path to reach a junction, with a clearing to your left. Walk through the clearing to the main gravel track.

3 Turn left and continue for 600yds (549m) to a gate and the turn-off for the lake, Point **2**. About 30 paces after the gate, head right up a signed footpath along the edge of a small copse, keeping the fence to your right. At the top of this wood, 30 paces off the track to your left is a disused mineshaft.

4 Continue up the track and straight ahead to Apedale, a former mining community. On the right, just after the track veers to the left, is Gamekeeper's Cottage, once the site of a colliery.

5 About 100yds (91m) beyond the cottage turn left and go over a stile by a gate. Cross the field ahead to reach another stile. Go left to yet another stile, head right following a fence to the bottom of the hill, then skirt left to reach another stile.

6 Cross into Watermills Wood and follow the trail to another stile, then come to a junction of two paths. Head right here and, after 10 paces, fork right again. You'll shortly come to a succession of stiles before continuing up to Watermills Farm.

7 Go over a stile and continue for 100yds (91m) before following a footpath left over a series of fields and stiles to some farm buildings on your right. When the fence veers round to the left, follow it to the edge of a young plantation. At the wide gravel track, head right and at a fork go left to reach the summit and the preserved pit wheel and wagon.

8 From the summit drop down the other side, continuing over a crossroads for a gently curving track to a T-junction. Head right here, and then take the wide track left down the hill. At the tarmac road head left and continue back towards the Heritage Centre.

WHERE TO EAT AND DRINK The Heritage Centre cafe, conveniently situated at the start of the walk, sells a variety of drinks and snacks and is open daily 10am–4pm.

WHAT TO SEE The highlight of the walk is undoubtedly the view from the hilltop at Point **8**, where a wide circle of carved wooden posts indicates the position of various distant landmarks on the horizon, such as Mow Cop Castle, 6 miles (9.7km) to the north (see Walk 6), and Pye Green Mast, 25 miles (40km) to the south on Cannock Chase. The scene is relatively pollution-free today, and it's hard to imagine that the view to the east was once shrouded in smog, or that 'smoky postcards' were once very popular as a souvenir of the times when plenty of smoke meant plenty of work.

WHILE YOU'RE THERE By the Heritage Centre at the start of the walk is Apedale Valley Light Railway, which opened in 2010 and will eventually run for about a mile (1.6km) into the Country Park. The narrow-gauge line has steam trains and diesels running throughout the year – see www.avlr.org.uk.

Ilam and the River Manifold

DISTANCE 4.75 miles (7.7km)	**MINIMUM TIME** 2hrs 15min	

ASCENT/GRADIENT 607ft (185m) ▲▲▲   **LEVEL OF DIFFICULTY** ✦✦✦

PATHS Metalled roads, parkland, open hillside and woods, many stiles

LANDSCAPE Parkland, woodland and hillside

SUGGESTED MAP AA Leisure Map 7 Central Peak District

START/FINISH Grid reference: SK131507

DOG FRIENDLINESS Keep on lead near livestock

PARKING At Ilam Hall (National Trust pay car park)

PUBLIC TOILETS At Ilam Hall

The Manifold and Dove rivers were both fished by Izaak Walton, known as the 'Father of Angling' and the author of *The Compleat Angler*, or *The Contemplative Man's Recreation*. Since the first edition appeared in 1653 it has never been out of print.

IZAAK WALTON

Born in Stafford in 1593, Walton moved to London as an apprentice ironmonger, becoming a craftsman and guild member when he was 25 years old. For most of his working life he owned an ironmongers shop in Fleet Street and lived in a house in Chancery Lane. A keen angler, he spent much of his spare time fishing on the Thames, but it was not until retirement that he was able to devote himself to his hobby completely. 'I have laid aside business, and gone a-fishing.'

SHREWD OPERATOR

The view we have of Walton from his book is of a genial old buffer strolling along river banks in pastoral England. But nothing could be further from the truth. Walton lived during a period of political upheaval and unrest. In 1649 he saw the execution of Charles I, and left London for Staffordshire, where he stayed during the Civil War. A staunch Royalist, he is mentioned among the supporters of Charles II after the Battle of Worcester in 1651. Following the battle he visited a friend who had been imprisoned in Stafford. From this friend Walton received the King's ring, which he delivered to Colonel Blague, then a prisoner in the Tower of London. The Colonel escaped, made his way to France and returned the ring to the King. If caught, Walton would have been executed. Just two years after 'the only know adventure' in his life he published his famous book.

CELEBRATED WORK

The Compleat Angler is the story of three sportsmen – Viator, a huntsman, Auceps, a fowler and Piscator, the fisherman – walking the River Lea on May Day, debating the finer points of their chosen sport. The fifth edition in 1676 contained an addition by Walton's friend and fishing companion, Charles Cotton, who lived at Beresford Hall near Hartington. Cotton built a little fishing house on the banks of the Dove near his home, which still stands today. This 'holy shrine for all anglers' has the interlacing initials of both men and the inscription 'Piscatoribus Scarum 1674'.

Following the restoration of the monarchy and Charles II, Walton moved to Winchester as the guest of his friend George Morley, Bishop of Winchester, and lived there until he died, aged 90 on 15 December, 1683. He was buried in the floor of the Chapel of St John the Evangelist and the Fisherman Apostles.

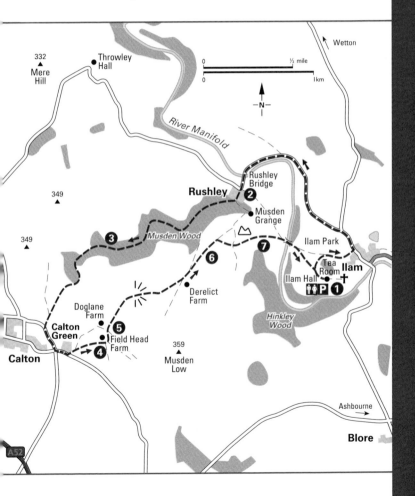

1 Leave the car park from the corner (pedestrian exit), turn right through a gate and follow the track through the park around to the right. Cross a stile and turn left onto the road out of Ilam village. Go uphill and turn left at Park Cottage onto the Castern and Throwley road. At a Y-junction go left, following the road across Rushley Bridge.

2 Go through Rushley Farm and then turn right, through a gate beside the sheep pens and before the drive up to Musden Grange. Go ahead to cross a stile, and continue ahead following the waymarked path beside a stone wall and a fence, walking along the valley bottom through woodland and then several fields.

3 Go over a series of stiles and gates and, at the final one, turn left onto the road. At the crossroads turn left towards Ashbourne. Go left through a gate at the next public footpath sign and cross the field. Cross a stile, go half left through another field to a stile to the left of a farm, then head diagonally left across the next field.

4 Cross the wall by stone steps, and head diagonally right to a gap stile to the right of some buildings. Continue on this line to a gate in the hedge to the right of Field Head Farm onto the road. Follow this round the boundary of the farm and go over a stile on the right by a metal gate.

5 Follow the field-edge path uphill. Go through a gate, cross the field to where two walls meet at a corner and follow the wall to the right. Join a farm road, pass a derelict farmstead, then turn diagonally right across a field and through a gap stile in the wall at the far corner.

6 Follow the direction pointer past two marker stones to the next public footpath sign and go right. Follow the wall on your right, go through a gap and veer diagonally left downhill, aiming just to the left of the pointed hill (Thorpe Cloud) ahead.

7 Go across two fields, a stile and then a bridge and into Ilam Park. Turn right and at the gate fork left, uphill, on a broad track that crosses the grounds back to the car park.

WHERE TO EAT AND DRINK The National Trust's Manifold Tea Room, located above the shop and overlooking the terraced gardens of Ilam Hall, provides welcome refreshment. It's open at weekends throughout the year and daily in the summer; look out for tasty treats such as apricot flapjack, chocolate orange fudge cake and cream teas. There is a large area of outside seating that allows terrific views across the park.

WHAT TO SEE As you cross Ilam Park try and pick out the well-preserved remains of medieval ridge and furrow fields on the right-hand side. Look for the track that runs across them. It was once used by local tradesmen and servants at Ilam Hall who were forbidden to use the main drive.

WHILE YOU'RE THERE Visit the church that stands in the grounds of Ilam Hall. Originally Norman, it was rebuilt in the 19th century but retains some of its older features. Inside is an elaborate and striking monument depicting the deathbed scene of David Pike Watts, with his only daughter and her children.

Around Caldonlow

DISTANCE 6 miles (9.7km)	**MINIMUM TIME** 2hrs 30min

ASCENT/GRADIENT 480ft (146m) ▲▲▲   **LEVEL OF DIFFICULTY** ✚✚✚

PATHS Field and woodland paths, can be muddy, many stiles

LANDSCAPE Farmland, quarry and hilltop

SUGGESTED MAP AA Leisure Map 7 Central Peak District

START/FINISH Grid reference: SK086494

DOG FRIENDLINESS Must be kept on lead near livestock

PARKING Roadside parking at start point near cement works

PUBLIC TOILETS None on route (nearest at Waterhouses car park by cycle hire centre)

The story of Caldonlow begins around 350 million years ago. Thanks to the whims of continental drift, the North Staffordshire moorlands and the Peak District of Derbyshire were much further south than they are today, and the region was covered by a shallow tropical sea. Over millions of years, a layer of shells and coral slowly built up on the seabed, both formed from the calcium carbonate secretions of a variety of marine animals.

THE CREATION OF LIMESTONE

As there was little current to disturb these deposits, this layer was slowly compacted by additional layers of sediment, again over millions of years, to create limestone. Chalk, marble and limestone are all calcium carbonate, each made under different conditions. Limestone is in fact almost pure calcium carbonate and as a result is very light in colour (hence the name White Peak, as opposed to the gritstone areas of the Dark Peak further north).

QUARRIES

In places like the White Peak, subsequent weathering, erosion and the ice age scoured away the softer topsoil leaving the limestone outcrops at or near the surface, which could then be readily quarried. This is what happened at Caldonlow Quarry, which at the height of the Industrial Revolution yielded some 6,000 tons a week. The limestone was transported on a tramway to the terminus of the Caldon Canal at Froghall, 3 miles (4.8km) west, and from there it was taken by barge to Stoke, Macclesfield and other canal-fed towns across the Midlands.

High-quality stone was used directly for building, while aggregate (crushed stone) was used for making roads. When calcium carbonate is heated, it leaves a deposit of calcium oxide or quicklime. Quicklime is even more useful than limestone. As a fertiliser it improves crop yields by reducing the acidity of soil, and it also reacts with the main impurities in iron ore to make iron and calcium silicate (or slag), which floats on top of the molten iron and is removed for use in road building.

A SITE OF SPECIAL SCIENTIFIC INTEREST

At Froghall, the limestone was fired in kilns to produce quicklime. The wharf and the kilns are long abandoned and the quarry is much quieter. It's now a designated geological Site of Special Scientific Interest and is dominated by the massive cement works at the start of the walk.

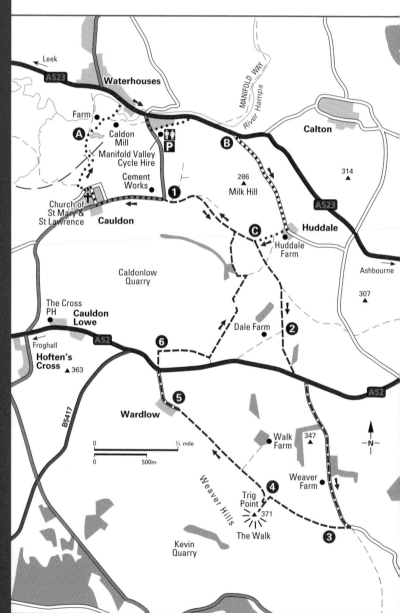

1 From the road corner head east along the gravel track, walking away from Cauldon. At the first corner go straight on for a track along a small valley. Pass a barn on your right, go through a slot or swing gate and then take the right fork along a wide dirt track. Go through the second gate ahead of you and after 25 paces go right, through an overgrown area, for a small stile into a wide, sloping field. Carry on straight up the hill.

2 At the far top corner of the field, go through a gate and straight across the next field to a gap in the wall ahead. After the gap, head for the far left-hand corner of the next field and cross a stile onto the A52. Bear left for 100yds (91m), then turn right along the narrow metalled road past Weaver Farm. As the road veers to the left it meets a fence. Go right, back on yourself, up the hill towards a gate in the dry-stone wall.

3 After crossing the stile here keep following the dry-stone wall to your right. At the next gate continue in the same direction, with the wall to your left. At the end of this wall bear slightly right to join another wall on the right and follow it to the gate.

4 Before crossing the dry-stone wall ahead, go left for 100yds (91m) and then right over a stile, before making straight for the trig point. From the trig point retrace your steps to the stile, but instead of crossing it, head left across the field, making for the dry-stone wall at the bottom. Follow this wall all the way to Wardlow.

5 Continue as far as the A52 and go straight across, following a public footpath sign. Continue over the thistly plateau of this field to a stile.

6 Turn right, go over another stile and along a waymarked route through the narrow belt of trees. At the far end go ahead through newly planted trees. Cross the stile in the far right corner and go left between the fence and wall. At the second stile turn right and go down the field-edge to a stile. Go left for 100yds (91m) and then right along a trail through a narrow valley. At the bottom of the valley rejoin the main track to return to the start point.

WHERE TO EAT AND DRINK The Cross at Cauldon Lowe is a 17th-century free house and restaurant. It serves a variety of real ales and fine home-cooked food at lunchtimes and evenings, daily.

WHAT TO SEE The trig point on the summit has expansive views out over South Staffordshire. The ancient mound here indicates that this may have been used as a beacon for sending warning messages by bonfire in medieval times.

WHILE YOU'RE THERE Take a short bike ride along the Manifold Way (see Walk 8). Mountain bikes and tandems can be hired from Manifold Valley Cycle Hire at the Old Station Car Park at Waterhouses (open most weekends throughout the year, daily in summer). For more information visit the website at www.visitpeakdistrict.com/activities/cycling.aspx. Dove Dale, to the east of Waterhouses, is a very deep, steep, heavily wooded valley that offers great walking.

Waterhouses and the Manifold Way

DISTANCE 9 miles (14.5km)	MINIMUM TIME 3hrs 45min

ASCENT/GRADIENT 751ft (229m) ▲▲▲   LEVEL OF DIFFICULTY ✦✦✦

SEE MAP AND INFORMATION PANEL FOR WALK 18

From Point ❶, at the corner of the road, head west towards Cauldon village, up a gentle slope, passing the cement works on your right. Take the second right into the village (look out for an old water fountain with its whimsical poem carved into the stone just before the turning) and then continue up the hill as far as the Church of St Mary and St Lawrence. Turn left just after the church and then, after 100yds (91m), turn right along a wide gravel track. After another 100yds (91m), head right at a sharp left bend and follow the path round until it runs beside an old railway embankment dropping away to the left. Head left, over an overgrown bridge, and drop down the far side of the embankment to reach a wide gravel track, Point ❹.

Keep to the left of the lake. Beyond a stile by a wide gate turn right onto another track and follow the waymarkers to the left to find an overgrown path down to a farmyard. Keep to the right of the farm buildings for a driveway to Caldon Mill, and then left to reach the A523. Go right for 250yds (229m) through the quiet village of Waterhouses and then turn right (shortly going under a disused railway bridge) and then first left to Manifold Valley Cycle Hire and the start of the Manifold Way (see Walk 8) – the building is a part of the old station. Follow the cycle track until it drops down to reach the A523. Now turn right and walk along the pavement for 650 yards (594m).

At Point ❸ turn right along a quiet road and follow it as far as Huddale Farm. Turn right here along a track to regain the main route at Point ❸. Retrace your steps to the start.

WHAT TO SEE The River Hamps, which runs through Waterhouses alongside the A523, is often seen (or, more precisely, not seen) to be flowing underground. This is because the limestone bedrock is porous and in many places, particularly when the water levels are low, the river can disappear into so-called swallow holes to flow through underground channels, exposing the dry river bed of water-smoothed limestone.

Consall Nature Park

DISTANCE 3.5 miles (5.7km)   MINIMUM TIME 1hr 30min

ASCENT/GRADIENT 360ft (110m) ▲▲▲   LEVEL OF DIFFICULTY ✚✚✚

PATHS Gravel tracks, tow paths and roads, can be muddy, many stiles and steps

LANDSCAPE Canal, meadow and woodland

SUGGESTED MAP OS Explorers 258 Stoke-on-Trent; 259 Derby

START/FINISH Grid reference: SJ994483

DOG FRIENDLINESS Must be kept on lead in nature park

PARKING Consall Nature Park visitor centre

PUBLIC TOILETS At visitor centre

Consall Nature Park, like Dimmings Dale near Alton, is a part of the Churnet Valley and has a long industrial history. Iron working is known to have taken place here as early as the 13th century, when vast tracts of woodland were felled to provide charcoal for smelting. Later, towards the end of the 18th century, the place was mined for ironstone, and the arrival of the Caldon Canal and the Churnet Valley Railway meant it was once again stripped of trees to make way for progress. At its peak, 1,500 men worked here, filling 30 barges a day with iron ore that was shipped to the wharf at Froghall.

CANAL AND RAILWAY LINKS

Today this region has been largely reclaimed by nature, but many landmarks remain. The railway, for example, was built in 1849 to link Manchester and Macclesfield with the rest of the Midlands, transporting iron ore, coal and limestone all over the district. Although it stopped operating commercially in the 1960s, it has been given a new lease of life as a tourist attraction, and the once-derelict Consall Station has been lovingly restored. Before the arrival of the railway, the Caldon Canal served a similar purpose, and there are still giant lime kilns where the canal and the river meet. These kilns were used to burn limestone from the vast Caldonlow quarries near by to produce quicklime, which could then be used in fertiliser or mortar. Even The Black Lion pub was built in the early 1800s specially to serve the men who lived and worked in the area. To this day it's still not accessible by road. Back then, it could be reached only by a cart track, by the steep steps running up beside the kilns, by canal and, later, by rail.

WOODLAND COVER RETURNS TO THE VALLEY

At the top of the steps beside the kilns are the remnants of spoil heaps, but the further you go from the river, the harder it is to find evidence of the damage done in the name of progress. In 1994 the Consall Nature Park was designated as a Site of Special Scientific Interest, as the largest area of semi-natural woodland in Staffordshire. Today this region is dominated by birch trees, which are often the first to recover after deforestation. There are no large trees since these were felled when the original forest was cleared for charcoal, mining and railways, although there are signs that oak trees may be starting to establish themselves, protected in their youth by the silver birches. With the rejuvenated woodland has come the wildlife. In the spring the pool and wet flushes are home to newts, frogs, toads and dragonflies, while birds include not just seasonal visitors like pied flycatchers and redstarts, but also water-loving dippers and kingfishers. All three species of woodpecker can be found here, as well as treecreepers and nuthatches, scaling the trunks of trees in search of insects hidden in the bark.

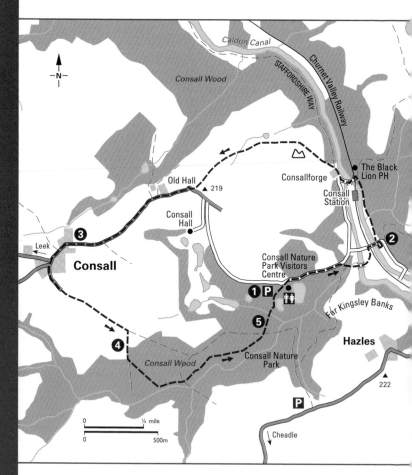

1 From the car park head to the left of the visitor centre to join a road. Go right and, at the far bottom of the road, bear diagonally right over a field to cross a footbridge. Follow the path right and then left to reach the corner of a bridge across a railway. Cross the bridge and go right down a set of steps.

2 Turn right and walk along the tow path. Soon after you pass Consall Station on your left, walk under the railway opposite The Black Lion pub and cross the canal and then the river. Just to the left of the lime kiln go up 204 steep steps and, at the top, walk right, along a grass track. At the brow of the hill follow the path to a gate and two little mounds. After picking your way through these mounds, cross the stile in the corner of the field and, after 30 paces, walk right via a stile. Head diagonally left across this field to cross a stile and continue on the track. At the metalled road go right and follow it towards Consall.

3 After 600yds (549m) reach a black-and-white timbered farmhouse on your right in the village of Consall. Just after a T-junction (signposted to Leek) go left across a farmyard following a signed public footpath. Cross a stile, continue along the wide track to another stile, then follow a line of trees just to your left-hand side. Carry on through a series of stiles to the corner of a wood.

4 In the wood carry straight on, ignoring the trail to your left. When the path you're on bears left, follow it to cross a stile back into Consall Nature Park. Go straight down the hill, again ignoring a path to the left. At the bottom, head left along the wider track. When this joins an even wider grassy track, bear right and continue straight on, ignoring paths to the left and right.

5 By a water outpipe, follow the track round to the right, then go left at the fork, pass a fishing lake to your right and return to the visitor centre.

WHERE TO EAT AND DRINK The Black Lion, in the heart of the Churnet Valley, is a great place for a pie and pint. It does the usual bar snacks and has an extensive restaurant menu. Food is served daily in summer.

WHAT TO SEE At the pond by the visitor centre, look out for resident water voles. They're not the most outgoing of animals and their burrow – a nest made of rushes and grass – is often below the surface. You should be able to see signs of their existence, from tracks in the mud to the nibbled tops of pond plants.

WHILE YOU'RE THERE Spend some time in Consall Nature Park Visitor Centre: it has a touch table, interactive displays, and information on both the industrial and natural history of the area. It also sells cold drinks and snacks.

Overleaf: A bridge over the Caldon Canal (Walk 20)

Froghall Wharf and the Churnet Valley

DISTANCE 4.5 miles (7.2km)	**MINIMUM TIME** 2hrs 15min	

ASCENT/GRADIENT 650ft (198m) ▲▲▲   **LEVEL OF DIFFICULTY** +++

PATHS Grass paths and dirt tracks may be muddy and slippery in very wet weather; many stiles and steep steps

LANDSCAPE Forest and farmland

SUGGESTED MAP OS Explorer 259 Derby

START/FINISH Grid reference: SK027477

DOG FRIENDLINESS Keep on lead near livestock

PARKING Froghall Wharf car park

PUBLIC TOILETS At Froghall Wharf picnic site

These days Froghall Wharf is a very pleasant and secluded picnic site at the heart of North Staffordshire's Churnet Valley, but this hasn't always been the case. In 1777 the Caldon Canal from Stoke-on-Trent to Froghall was completed by engineering whizz James Brindley. Froghall was chosen as the site for the eastern terminus of the canal because of its proximity to the limestone quarries situated at Caldonlow, just 3 miles (4.8km) to the east.

TRANSPORTING LIMESTONE

In theory, the limestone could have been taken from the quarry to Froghall on a basic tramway and then loaded onto barges bound for Stoke-on-Trent. In practice however, the quarries were some 680ft (207m) higher than the canal, which meant building the tramway was almost as difficult as building the canal. The first version, built in 1778, soon proved to be inadequate. A replacement, completed in 1785, fared little better. A few years later, though, a third line was built and this was made more efficient by an ingenious device called a brake drum. Full wagons at the top of the incline were attached to empty wagons at the bottom via a large wooden drum; when these loaded wagons were rolled to the bottom, the empty wagons were pulled to the top, letting gravity do all the hard work.

AT THE WHARF

By the start of the 19th century, the tramway was delivering thousands of tons of limestone a week to Froghall Wharf. In the 1840s a fourth tramway was built, which followed a virtually straight line to the quarry. When the limestone reached the wharf it was either loaded directly onto barges to be taken to Stoke for use in construction, or it was fed into the tops of the enormous lime kilns that can still be seen at the wharf today. Layers of coal were added and then the mixture was fired to reduce the limestone to quicklime. This was collected at the bottom and taken to nearby farms for use as a fertiliser; it was also used in mortar and as an ingredient in smelting iron from iron ore.

SPECIAL SITE

Froghall Wharf has now been designated a Site of Special Scientific Interest (SSSI), thanks to its flower meadows and large areas of woodland, which support 50 species of birds, plus many more species of insects dependent on over-mature trees.

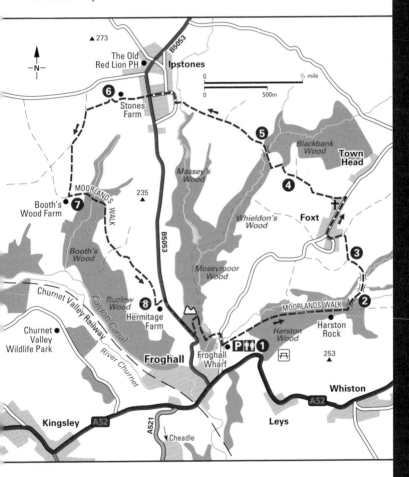

❶ From the car park go up a short ramp and along the gravel track ahead. At the fork head right and, just after Harston Rock, go left down a trail signed 'Moorlands Walk'. At the bottom cross a footbridge.

❷ Shortly after the footbridge, cross a stile and the bottom of a field. Once back in the woods again, cross another footbridge and go through a narrow stone slot. Continue across a field to a stile and another footbridge.

Cross another stile and follow a dry-stone wall up the hill.

3 At the top bear right and continue round, following the curve of the wall. After a wall gap, go down a gravel track to a surfaced road, then head right to the wide fork. Go right through Foxt, and after the church go hard left down a lane.

4 Just before a private drive go left and then at the end right, following the path along a fence. After crossing the stile continue through the wood to a small stream. Cross and shortly after go through a kissing gate and follow the path to a farm road.

5 Turn right to Ipstones. At the end, follow the footpath round to the left and then immediately up stone steps to the road. Follow the road right and then round to the left and, at the next corner, continue between the houses and along a road. At the main road go right then left along the footpath (signed) to Stones Farm.

6 Bear slightly to the left of the farm and, just past it, go over a stile on your right and then continue left along the track. Go through a gate and carry on to another. In the next field cross diagonally left to a gap in a hedge. Continue down the field to cross a stile in the far right corner. Keep on down the left-hand edge of this field to a track to Booth's Wood Farm, going left before the buildings into the field.

7 Cross a stile and head left, following the Moorlands Walk into Booth's Wood, and follow a stepped footpath down to a footbridge. At the top of the wood go over the stile and across the field to the corner of a dry-stone wall. Follow this wall and track to reach Hermitage Farm.

8 Go right on the main road and, after 400yds (366m), follow the footpath sign into the woods on the left. Follow this steep path down to a T-junction, then turn right to the canal. At the canal turn left towards the bridge, then cross it to reach the car park.

WHERE TO EAT AND DRINK If you want to stop halfway try The Old Red Lion in Ipstones. It serves hot and cold food in the evenings, Monday to Friday, and all day at weekends, and has a range of real ales, including Theakstons beer.

WHAT TO SEE As you leave the car park behind at the start you're actually walking along the line of the fourth and final tramway built between Froghall and Caldonlow. It followed an almost straight line between the two, and the cuttings and embankments that made this possible can still be see higher up the track.

WHILE YOU'RE THERE The Kingsley Bird and Falconry Centre, high above the Churnet Valley less than a mile (1.6km) west of Froghall, features a collection of more than 70 birds of prey, including rare owls and other raptors that you can see close up. There is also a small tea room serving hot and cold drinks, light snacks and refreshments. Guided tours around the centre take place daily from Easter to October and at weekends only in the winter. For more details go to www.kingsleyfalconry.co.uk.

Ellastone and Calwich Abbey

DISTANCE 4 miles (6.4km)	MINIMUM TIME 1hr 30min
ASCENT/GRADIENT 360ft (110m) ▲▲▲	LEVEL OF DIFFICULTY ✦✦✦
PATHS Gravel tracks, roads and grass trails, many stiles	
LANDSCAPE Farmland	
SUGGESTED MAP OS Explorer 259 Derby	
START/FINISH Grid reference: SK118426	
DOG FRIENDLINESS Must be kept on lead	
PARKING Ample parking along village roads	
PUBLIC TOILETS None on route	

Ellastone, near the Derbyshire border to the southwest of Ashbourne, is known for its literary and musical associations, both of which involve people named George, or so it would seem. The first is George Eliot, author of – among others – *Silas Marner* (1861) and *Middlemarch* (1871). Eliot's first novel *Adam Bede* is based on the village of Ellastone; in the book it is referred to as Hayslope, while Staffordshire is named Loamshire. When it was first published in 1859, by a completely unknown author, a number of impostors tried to claim authorship of the book. Only then was it revealed that George Elliot was a pen name for Marian Evans, who wrote for the prestigious *Westminster Review*.

A VICTORIAN SCANDAL

The scandal that broke when it was discovered that George Eliot was a woman was exacerbated by the fact that she was also having an extramarital affair with George Henry Lewis, her editor. Unable to divorce his faithless wife, George Henry entered into a common-law marriage with George Eliot. Polite Victorian society was far too conservative for such sordid behaviour, and the author was ostracised by her family and friends. This rejection became one of the themes of her next novel, *The Mill on the Floss*, published in 1860.

REFLECTING THE REAL WORLD

As for *Adam Bede*, its success then, as now, lay in Eliot's ability to reflect everyday life in her characters and the worlds they inhabited. Shunning the romanticism prevalent in the first half of the 19th century, she was one of the first writers to insist on realism, believing that novels should reflect not only the real world, but also some underlying moral purpose above and beyond the entertainment to be had from a good read. In *Adam Bede*, the hero is thought to have been based heavily on Marian's own father, and in amongst a tragic love story – interlaced with rich descriptions of rural life – lies the novel's central theme, that selflessness is the secret of happiness.

A GREAT COMPOSER

The second George to find inspiration in Ellastone was George Frideric Handel (1685–1759). His most famous work is arguably *The Messiah*, which he composed while staying with friends at Calwich Abbey in 1741 (Calwich Abbey is passed in the early stages of the walk). *The Messiah* was first performed, in aid of charity, in Dublin a year later, where it was met with rapturous applause. Some years later, King George II was so moved on hearing the *Hallelujah Chorus* that he rose to his feet; the audience duly followed his example and the tradition remains today, even in the absence of royalty.

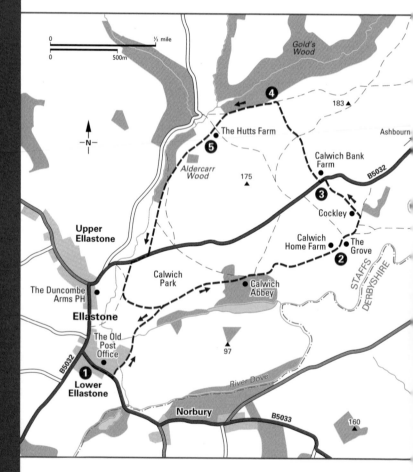

1 From the former post office, opposite the red post box, go left and then take the first left down an obvious gravel track. Keep going straight to Calwich Abbey. Follow the track left of the abbey and along the metalled road as far as Calwich Home Farm.

2 Pass the farm and follow the track round to the left of The Grove and through a gate. At the fork go left, through another gate and down a slope and, after 50yds (46m), veer left off the track up a short hill to a stile in front of Cockley farm. Cross the stile and head just to the right of Cockley, following a dirt and grass track all the way to the B5032.

3 At the road go left and then first right, through Calwich Bank Farm and up a gravel track. When the track bears round to the right, keep going straight into a field, making for a gap in the hedge at the top right-hand corner. Go through the gap, over a stile on the left and then follow the hedge left, down the field.

4 At the bottom follow the hedge round to the left and cut diagonally right across the field to a stile. After crossing the stile, skirt round the top of the wood to another stile and continue as far as The Hutts Farm. After a stile take the gravel track up the hill to a gate into the farmyard and head straight on to another stile into a field.

5 Continue straight across, making for the corner of Aldercarr Wood ahead to the left. Keep going straight on and down to the far bottom corner of the field, and carry on along the right-hand edge of the next field. At the far end cross another stile and continue straight on (not diagonally left) to the B5032. Turn right along the road and, after 100yds (91m), take the path to the left. Head diagonally right across the field to a double stile and then left round the bottom of a small mound with trees. Keep going as far as the junction of the two bridleways, between Point **1** and Point **2**, and from here retrace your steps back to the start.

WHERE TO EAT AND DRINK The Duncombe Arms in Ellastone serves a range of meals and snacks, plus traditional beers at lunchtime and evenings throughout the week.

WHAT TO SEE Sadly, little remains of the abbey – founded in 1148 – where Handel once penned his greatest work, *The Messiah*, in 24 days, and not much remains of Calwich Hall, which was built in its place. All that can be seen today is a disused stable block and a fishing temple by the lake.

WHILE YOU'RE THERE Ashbourne is a picturesque and predominantly Georgian market town near the edge of the Peak District, and is well worth a visit. Market days are Thursday and Saturday, but its best tradition is surely the Royal Shrovetide Football Match, when the Up'ards (those from north of the Henmore Brook) play the Down'ards (those from the south) using a pitch where the goals are 3 miles (4.8km) apart. The game is played with a specially made and painted ball, and can last until 10pm, flowing back and forth through the town.

Around Alton

DISTANCE 5 miles (8km)   MINIMUM TIME 2hrs

ASCENT/GRADIENT 361ft (110m) ▲▲▲   LEVEL OF DIFFICULTY ✦✦✦

PATHS Roads, gravel tracks and dirt trails; many stiles on Walk 24

LANDSCAPE Forest and farmland

SUGGESTED MAP OS Explorer 259 Derby

START/FINISH Grid reference: SK073423

DOG FRIENDLINESS Can be off lead in woods

PARKING Parking on Alton village roads

PUBLIC TOILETS None on route

Alton has more than its fair share of history, not to mention a name that's practically synonymous with stomach-churning, roller-coaster rides. The first recorded settlement in the area was an Iron Age fort on Bunbury Hill – site of present-day Alton Towers – built before 1000 BC. In the eighth century AD it was a fortress for the Saxon king Coelred, and in the 12th century it was given to a soldier by the name of Bertram de Verdun, as thanks for the part he played in the Crusades.

A CONSPICUOUS CASTLE

In 1176 de Verdun built a castle high above the Churnet Valley, on the opposite side to the original fort. The castle remains are at the start of the walk but are on the site of a children's centre, so you can only glimpse the ruined tower and walls. A sheer cliff lies below the north side, and on the east and south sides is a deep ditch. The lower parts of a wall remain, as does most of a rectangular tower and the base of a round tower. The castle was held for King Charles in the Civil War but later dismantled by Parliament to stop it being used by Royalists.

Opposite the castle is the present-day Catholic Youth Centre, begun in 1847 to a design by A W Pugin, who was partly responsible for the Houses of Parliament. Originally a private home, it was used as a boarding school from 1919 until 1989; and has been a youth centre since 1995.

While Pugin was rebuilding the estate, successive generations of the Talbot family began to rebuild the landscape, especially the area of Dimmings Dale to the west of Alton. Ore smelting had flourished in the valley for 150 years but by 1850 the industry was gone. Hillsides had been stripped of trees to fire smelting furnaces, spoil heaps littered the valley and the stream had been dammed to provide water to operate the smelting mill. Today, thanks to the Talbot family, the forest has been restored and the spoil heaps are gone, but the lakes and the original mill still remain as part of a peaceful forest walk.

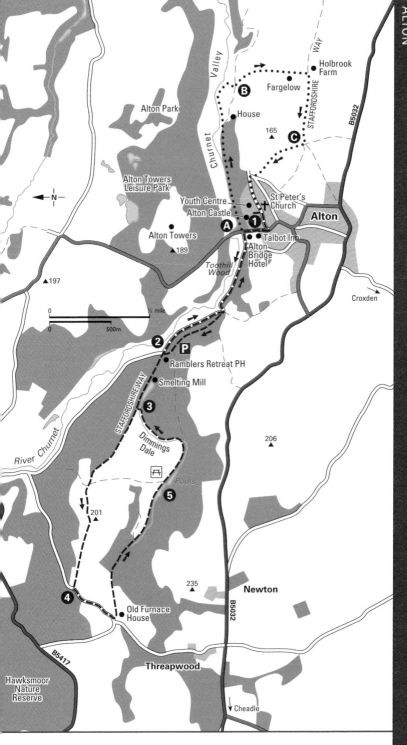

Holbrook Farm
Fargelow
House
STAFFORDSHIRE WAY
Churnet Valley
Alton Park
165
B5032
Alton Towers Leisure Park
Alton Towers
▲189
Youth Centre
Alton Castle
St Peter's Church
Alton
Talbot Inn
Alton Bridge Hotel
Toothill Wood
▲197
Croxden
0   ½ mile
0   500m
Ramblers Retreat PH
Smelting Mill
STAFFORDSHIRE WAY
Dimmings Dale
Pools
River Churnet
206
▲201
235
Newton
Old Furnace House
B5032
B5417
Hawksmoor Nature Reserve
Threapwood
↓ Cheadle

1 At the castle gate, head straight down the track to the right of St Peter's Church. At the main road, head right, down the hill to the river and the Alton Bridge Hotel. Head left along a metalled road, past the hotel, going straight ahead where the road goes round to the left, along the base of Toothill Wood. Just after the road goes round an obvious hairpin bend, follow a wide track into the woods on the left, shown by a public bridleway sign. After 400yds (366m) go right off the track down a less obvious trail to Dimmings Dale car park and the Ramblers Retreat pub.

2 Go through the car park to the right of the pub, then straight on, following signs for the Staffordshire Way. Pass the smelting mill and lake on your left, and continue straight on at the end of the lake, staying to the right of the impressive stone house.

3 When you climb up to a path junction amid the open woods,

go straight over, following more Staffordshire Way signs, and still ascending. At the top of the hill go right along the metalled road, over a cattle grid, and follow this road all the way to a T-junction.

4 Go left at the junction and, after 400yds (366m), go left again just before Old Furnace House. When you get to a fork in the track, head right, close to the stream and past a series of pools, until you get to a picnic table and a causeway between two pools.

5 Continue to the left of the stream after the final pool, staying on the left at the first wooden footbridge. When you get to a dry-stone wall barring the way straight ahead, go right over a wooden footbridge and continue to follow the river left. This path will shortly bring you back to the smelting mill and the Ramblers Retreat. From there head along the road back to the hotel and then retrace your steps back to St Peter's Church.

WHERE TO EAT AND DRINK The Ramblers Retreat pub is in a very secluded spot in the heart of the Churnet Valley, just a few minutes' walk from Dimmings Dale. The food, ranging from cakes and snacks right through to three-course meals, is invariably excellent. It's open daily, 10am–5pm in July and August, 10am–4pm from September to June.

WHAT TO SEE The old smelting mill is now a private residence and it's hard to see any detail, but the original waterwheel is still there and you can't miss the necklace of pools that stretches up the valley. The mill was built in 1741 and was used for smelting lead ore. After the decline of the smelting industry near the end of the century, it was converted to a corn mill, its 20ft (6m) wheel driving three pairs of grinding stones.

WHILE YOU'RE THERE The Hawksmoor Nature Reserve has been in existence since 1927. It was originally the site of an iron-smelting furnace, and at Gibridding you can still see the remains of an inclined plane which was once a tramway used for hauling coal from the extensive mines at Cheadle to the Froghall-to-Uttoxeter canal. The wood is a haven for insects and birds, including spotted flycatchers in summer and occasional buzzards in winter.

The Churnet Valley

DISTANCE 7 miles (11.3km)   MINIMUM TIME 3hrs

ASCENT/GRADIENT 233ft (71m) ▲ ▲ ▲   LEVEL OF DIFFICULTY ✚ ✚ ✚

SEE MAP AND INFORMATION PANEL FOR WALK 23

From the Alton Bridge Hotel car park go right, Point **A**, across the main road, and follow a wide gravel track along the Churnet Valley. After 0.5 miles (800m), follow a footpath sign off the main track to the left just before a private drive. Take the path down to the river and then follow the river around to the right, ignoring a footbridge. Just before the river bears left again, head right, straight up the bank to a stile across the track, Point **B**.

After the stile, cross the track and go straight up the steep slope ahead, through a gap in the rocky outcrop. Near the top of this short slope, bear slightly left to a small stile and then head diagonally left across the field to its top left corner. Cross over the stile before heading right and then go straight up the field, keeping a hedge just to your right. At the top of this field go right through the gate and then left over a stile hidden in the hedge at the far end of the gate. After this stile, continue up the hedge as far as the ruins of Fargelow farm. Carry on to the left of this building to a gate at Holbrook Farm.

Through the gate, head right along a wide, grassy track (there's a slab path on the right which avoids any mud). After 600yds (549m), just before you get to a building, you reach two stiles, one to the left and one right, Point **C**. Follow the Staffordshire Way signpost right into a field, then skirt around the right-hand edge. At the top of this field go straight across the stile and, at the end of this field, follow it round to the left for 20 paces to get to the well-hidden stile. After the stile, head diagonally left across the field to a pair of stiles in the corner of the field.

At the road head right and, when you get to the big stone barn straight head, turn left, following the road down to Alton Castle and St Peter's Church.

WHILE YOU'RE THERE Founded at the end of the 12th century, Croxden Abbey was one of the last Cistercian abbeys to be built in England, and its architecture is more elaborate than earlier monasteries built by this strict order. The east end was unusually ornate, consisting of five chapels radiating from an ambulatory, of which only fragments now remain. The massive west front dominates the ruins, with rich mouldings around the middle doorway and three slender windows.

Dunstall Hall

DISTANCE 3.5 miles (5.7km)	**MINIMUM TIME** 2hrs

ASCENT/GRADIENT 344ft (105m) ▲▲▲   **LEVEL OF DIFFICULTY** ✚✚✚

PATHS Grassy field paths, dirt tracks and lanes, several stiles

LANDSCAPE Woods, parkland and fields

SUGGESTED MAP OS Explorer 245 The National Forest

START/FINISH Grid reference: SK186187

DOG FRIENDLINESS Keep on lead around livestock

PARKING Public car park by village hall, Barton-under-Needwood

PUBLIC TOILETS By car park

The centrepiece of this walk is Dunstall Hall, dating from the 1800s but replacing a much earlier building that once stood on the site of nearby Old Hall farm. Still privately owned, the hall and 1,000-acre (405ha) estate have passed through many different pairs of hands over the centuries, including those of Sir Richard Arkwright, son of the famous inventor of the world's first water-powered cotton spinning mill. After his father died he sold most of the family's mills, invested in landed property like Dunstall, and made his own personal fortune, so much so that on his death in 1842 he left over £3 million in his will (£150 million in today's money).

NEW WOODLAND COVER

In 2001 the owners of Dunstall Estate, Sir Stanley and Lady Hilda Clarke, began a tree-planting scheme as part of the wider National Forest programme. In the last five years alone more 180,000 trees have been planted and a series of new permissive paths has been established for visitors to enjoy. You will walk through the young woodland early on in the walk after leaving Barton-under-Needwood; and also part of the newly created Douglas Wood beyond Old Hall farm. The National Forest covers over 200sq miles (518sq km) of Staffordshire, Derbyshire and Leicestershire and has increased tree cover by 12 per cent in just 20 years. The plan is ultimately to plant 30 million trees and cover a third of the forest area. However, alongside the new planting, the National Forest also incorporates the little that remains of the ancient woodland of Staffordshire's Needwood Forest (which once spread to Barton – hence its name). There are walks galore and events throughout the year for all the family right across the National Forest, see www.nationalforest.org.

NOT SO SILLY WICKET

Near Dunstall Hall you pass the home of Dunstall Cricket Club and one of the most picturesque cricket grounds in the county. The club was founded in the 1890s and, despite its rural setting, boasts four senior sides and some real talent. It plays in the county's premier cricket league, and past club professionals have included former England legends Derek Randall and Devon Malcolm. If a match is under way, why not call in and enjoy some quintessential English village sport?

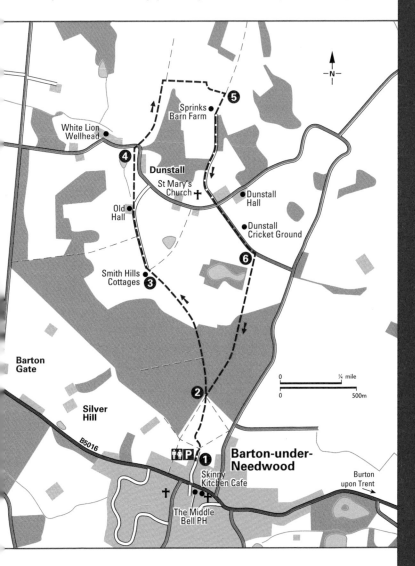

1 From the car park turn left along Crowberry Lane, past the Methodist Church. Go through a gate onto a wide farm track, then over a stile and ahead to an information panel. Go through the gate and straight ahead through the field to reach a solitary post.

2 Veer half left to go through a gate into woodland. Stay on the main path, ignoring permissive routes off to the left and the right, then via another gate walk out across a wide field. Bear slightly left to reach Smith Hills Cottages.

3 Go through two gates and across a lane for a track into a field. Where it meets a surfaced lane go straight on. With the entrance to Old Hall on your left go over a stile ahead and through a meadow, aiming for the gate in the far right corner. Continue on a path to reach a road.

4 Cross the road carefully for a stile opposite. Walk along the right edge of the field for 440yds (402m) until you get to a waymarker post. Turn right and walk down across the field, through a belt of trees and up across another field towards farm buildings. Aim for the metal gate between large sheds and go through this to cross the farmyard. Go through a gate for a double stile onto a lane.

5 Turn right and follow the lane past Sprinks Barn Farm as it becomes a surfaced drive. At the crossroads at the bottom of the hill, with the church on your right, go straight over, past the cricket ground, as far as a bend.

6 Turn right over a stile for a fenced path past an overgrown old pool. Continue through woodland to the gate at the far end. Go ahead through the field to the solitary post, then veer slightly left on the route back to the start.

WHERE TO EAT AND DRINK The Middle Bell is located near the start of the walk in Barton-under-Needwood and won the 2012 Taste of Staffordshire Good Food Award for the Best Traditional Pub and Restaurant. Food is served at lunchtimes and evenings and all day at weekends. For lighter snacks try the equally excellent Skinny Kitten Cafe on Main Street.

WHAT TO SEE At Point **4** you can deviate from the route by heading left up the lane for 100yds (91m) to visit the White Lion. Despite its name this isn't a pub, but an ornate stone wellhead carved to celebrate Queen Victoria's Jubilee and which for many years provided local people with drinking water. The Arkwright family's wealth paid for St Mary's Church in Dunstall. The pulpit is built from Caen stone, but the chancel is much more local, lined with alabaster from nearby Hanbury.

WHILE YOU'RE THERE A few miles to the south, off the A38 near Alrewas, is the National Memorial Arboretum. Opened in 2001, it's the UK's permanent centre of remembrance where more than 50,000 trees have been planted and 200 memorials established to commemorate members of the armed forces and civil services. The arboretum is free to enter and open year-round.

Loggerheads

DISTANCE 5.5 miles (8.8km)	**MINIMUM TIME** 2hrs

ASCENT/GRADIENT 240ft (73m) ▲▲▲   **LEVEL OF DIFFICULTY** ✦✦✦

PATHS Gravel tracks, roads and grass trails, many stiles

LANDSCAPE Woodland and farmland

SUGGESTED MAP OS Explorer 243 Market Drayton

START/FINISH Grid reference: SJ738359

DOG FRIENDLINESS Keep on lead near livestock

PARKING Ample parking in Loggerheads village

PUBLIC TOILETS None on route

Loggerhead, meaning 'blockhead' or 'fool,' is believed to be derived from the word 'logger', which was used colloquially to refer to a block of wood for hobbling horses. Loggerheads itself takes its name from the Loggerheads pub, formerly the Three Loggerheads, whose sign featured two fools' heads and a third, that of an onlooker.

WARS OF THE ROSES

It was at Bloreheath, west of the village, that the first major battle of the Wars of the Roses was fought. This involved an ongoing dispute between the House of Lancaster, led by King Henry VI, and the House of York, led by Richard, Duke of York. Richard believed he had a better claim to the throne than Henry and duly expected to inherit the crown; when the King sired a son and heir, however, Richard realised that he would have to resort to force.

QUEEN MARGARET

The year is 1459: Richard's allies are fragmented all over England, and to consolidate his forces he orders Neville, Earl of Salisbury, to march from Yorkshire to Ludlow, about 40 miles (64km) south of Bloreheath. Aware of this, Queen Margaret directs James Touchet, Lord Audley, to intercept Salisbury. Knowing that the road to Ludlow will take Salisbury through a defile near Bloreheath, Audley assembles 10,000 soldiers on the heath overlooking the road. On Sunday, 23 September, the two sides oppose each other across the valley. Salisbury is heavily outnumbered.

BATTLE TACTICS

Salisbury senses that Audley is over-confident and that he may be tempted into a glorious cavalry charge, to impress Queen Margaret and to destroy his enemy. To make it even more tempting, Salisbury feigns a retreat by withdrawing his pikemen from the front, leaving an opening for a charge. Seizing this opportunity, Audley orders his cavalry down the hill but underestimates the difficulty of ascending the steep, muddy slope of the brook at the bottom. Exposed and vulnerable, the horses are no match for Salisbury's archers, waiting in the wings. The result is unequivocal. Twice Audley's forces charge and twice they are mown down. A third assault involves more than 4,000 infantry. Audley is slain in the bitter hand-to-hand fighting which ensues, and today Audley's Cross still marks the spot where he died. The battle lasted all day. By nightfall, more than 2,000 Lancastrians lay dead or dying, while Yorkist casualties numbered just 56. But ultimately it was to no avail; after 30 years of war the Lancastrians kept the throne.

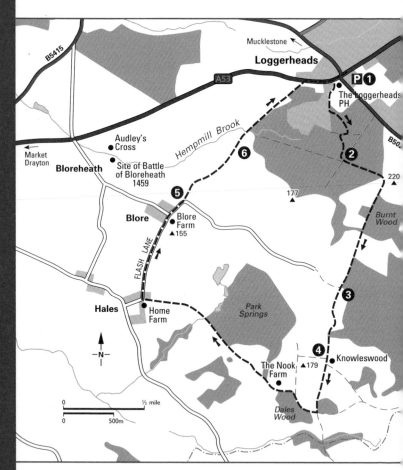

1 Head along the A53 in the direction of Market Drayton and take the first left along Kestrel Drive. Just after The Robins head left along the gravel track down the back of some houses. When you reach the end of a cul-de-sac, go left on a wide woodland track. After skirting a large, deep hollow turn right. At a clearing bear left past an iron bar across a wide track and, at the fork, go right, past the football pitch, then turn left uphill to reach a major path junction.

2 Take the fourth path on your left and where it bends left at the far end, follow a narrow path through the undergrowth ahead right to a gravel track. Turn right through the gate and continue for 0.5 miles (800m), until the main track goes right.

3 Head over a stile and along the footpath with a hedge to your right-hand side. At the bottom of the field bear right towards the right-hand corner of the bank of trees. Go through a gate here and head up towards Knowleswood farm (which is now derelict) and another gate.

4 Continue straight ahead and, at the bottom of the field, go right over a stile and drop down through a small dip. At the bottom of the dip go through a gate and head right along a concrete track. At a fork go left to The Nook Farm and, after a mile (1.6km) reach Home Farm. Turn right along the semi-surfaced Flash Lane and up the gentle hill to Blore Farm. When you get to a junction keep going

straight and, after 200yds (183m), head left through a hedge over a stile. Follow this hedge right to a stile in the bottom of the field. This stile probably provides the best vantage point from which to view the main battlefield, now private farm land, which was centred on the shallow valley to your left.

5 Continue to the bottom right-hand corner of the next field before bearing diagonally right across another field to the right-hand end of a bank of trees. Cross the small stile and follow the faint track straight across the middle of the next field to another stile.

6 Follow the path through a young plantation to a fence ahead and cross a stile. Keep following the faint track alongside a wood to your right and, when you come to a clearing, head diagonally across the field to the left-hand end of the trees. At the corner of this field, cross a stile and footbridge to a wide grassy track, which you follow right and up the hill to a large, lone oak at the top. Turn left here to cross a stile back onto the A53 to return to the start.

WHERE TO EAT AND DRINK The Loggerheads, at the start of the walk and in the centre of the village, is a popular pub that welcomes families. Food is served daily, including a Sunday carvery. There's extensive outdoor seating, and it even has its own woodland walks.

WHAT TO SEE Although it's difficult to actually walk across the battlefield today, the surrounding landscape still includes many of the same features that were present in 1459, such as lanes, villages, hedges and woodlands. Most obvious of these is Hempmill Brook, across which Audley's army charged. The site is one of a handful of medieval battlefields to have escaped modern development.

WHILE YOU'RE THERE It's said that Queen Margaret watched the defeat of the Lancastrian forces from the church tower at Mucklestone. Fearing for her safety, she made plans to flee, instructing the local blacksmith, William Skelhorn, to put the shoes on her horse the wrong way round, to disguise her escape. The anvil supposedly used by Skelhorn was preserved and still stands in front of St Mary's in Mucklestone.

Overleaf: Swynnerton's Italianate water tower (Walk 27)

The Hanchurch Hills

DISTANCE 7 miles (11.3km)	**MINIMUM TIME** 2hrs 30min

ASCENT/GRADIENT 420ft (128m) ▲▲▲   **LEVEL OF DIFFICULTY** ✛✛✛

PATHS Gravel tracks, field paths and roads

LANDSCAPE Woodland, farmland and village

SUGGESTED MAP OS Explorer 243 Market Drayton

START/FINISH Grid reference: SJ839399

DOG FRIENDLINESS Off-lead opportunities in woods and on fenced tracks

PARKING Hanchurch Hills Picnic Place car park

PUBLIC TOILETS None on route

The walk begins in Swynnerton Old Park, near the first of this walk's water towers. Of course, it's not just coincidence that there are so many water towers in the area; the sandstone strata of Meecebrook Valley, formed during the Triassic period, is capable of providing 1.5 million gallons (7 million litres) of clean water a day.

SATISFYING THE DEMAND FOR WATER

At the end of the 19th century, in response to an increase in demand for high-quality water, the Staffordshire Potteries Water Board built the Hatton Water Works, a project which took the best part of 20 years to complete. Water was pumped directly to Hanchurch Reservoir (now Hanchurch Pools), which then supplied water to Newcastle, Stoke and the Trent Valley.

RESTORED TOWER

Today, water is still pumped at Hatton, but electricity has replaced steam and the Grade II-listed, yellow- and red-brick buildings have been converted into luxury apartments. The restored water tower just north of Swynnerton gives an idea of quite how impressive these Italianate-style buildings must once have been, with their red-brick columns, circular windows and triumphal archways superimposed on warm, yellow-brick facades. The Swynnerton tower itself has been ingeniously rebuilt as a house, with its vast windows and spiral staircase in the middle, up to the first floor.

HISTORIC BUILDINGS

Swynnerton, meanwhile, has more than its fair share of historic buildings for a village so small. The oldest of these is 13th-century St Mary's Church. Apart from the statue of Christ (see What to See), the feature of most interest is undoubtedly the simple Norman doorway, which nonetheless has a detailed beakhead moulding. Over the road is a Roman Catholic church dedicated to Our Lady of the Assumption and built from local stone by Gilbert Blount, who tried to imbue his designs with a distinctly Gothic feel.

The chapel itself is attached to Swynnerton Hall. The hall was built in 1725 to replace an earlier manor house demolished by Cromwell in the Civil War. Its owner, Sir John Fitzherbert, supported the Royalist cause. His grandson Basil built the hall seen today.

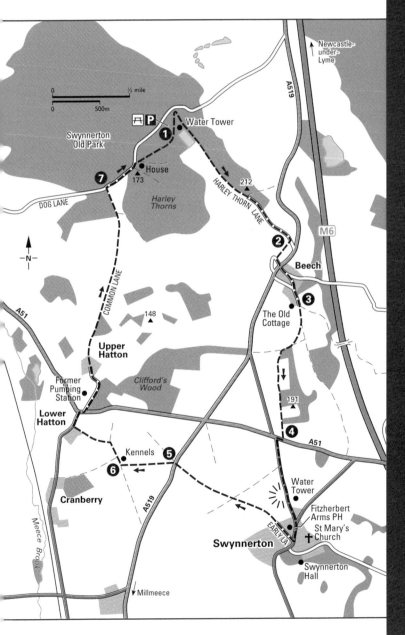

1 From the car park take the left fork along a gravel track, which is Harley Thorn Lane. Then veer left again at the next fork past a derelict water tower and reservoir on your right. After 650yds (594m) go through a gate and continue ahead along the metalled road.

2 Just before the A519 go right up a gravel track and, shortly after, at a hairpin in another road, head left, going downhill. At the next fork go right. At the road junction turn left and follow the road until you come to a fork just after The Old Cottage on your right.

3 Go right here and keep following the main path, ignoring the public footpath signs to the left. Where the obvious gravel bridleway veers left, head straight on and up into the woods. At the top of the woods carry straight on, following the track to the A51.

4 Turn right, then take the first left, following the minor road towards Swynnerton. Just past the Fitzherbert Arms on the right, turn right along Early Lane. At the end of the road, keep going straight along a signed footpath. At the far end, go straight on, in the same direction, across the middle of a wide field. Continue on this public footpath through three more fields to the A519.

5 Cross the road with care and then carry on by going left in the next field, beside the hedge. Continue to the end of the field, go through some trees and then right to the stile and a gravel drive.

6 Turn right past the kennels and, at Lower Hatton Stables, turn right along the road to the A51. Take care crossing this road, heading right then taking the first left, past Lower Hatton Pumping Station, now private residences. Follow this road to Upper Hatton and then carry on straight along Common Lane all the way back to Swynnerton Old Park.

7 At Dog Lane turn right and, after 400yds (366m), just beyond a house, turn right up a woodland path. Head left at the fork immediately after the start of the track. When you reach a clearing with a car park and picnic site, make for the left of the water tower, continuing along the track back to the start.

WHERE TO EAT AND DRINK The Fitzherbert Arms at Swynnerton is open at lunchtimes and evenings in the week and all day at weekends, and serves a range of meals and snacks. A little further afield try the coffee shop at Slater's Inn and Craft Village on the A51 at Hill Chorlton.

WHAT TO SEE The viewpoint in front of Swynnerton water tower has a good view over the Millbrook Valley and beyond. Also worth a look, if it's open, is St Mary's Church, which features an impressive statue of Christ dating from c.1260–80.

WHILE YOU'RE THERE The Mill Meece Pumping Station has supplied water to the Potteries since 1914. Two magnificent steam engines pumped more than 3 million gallons (13.6 million litres) of water a day. Today the water is pumped by electricity, but the preserved steam engines are fired up on steam weekends and other special occasions (small admission fee). The station is open most Sundays from 1–5pm.

Wedgwood Country

DISTANCE 3.25 miles (5.3km)   MINIMUM TIME 1hr 15min

ASCENT/GRADIENT 180ft (55m) ▲▲▲   LEVEL OF DIFFICULTY ✚✚✚

PATHS Roads, gravel tracks and tow paths

LANDSCAPE Village, farmland and canal

SUGGESTED MAP OS Explorer 258 Stoke-on-Trent

START/FINISH Grid reference: SJ889395

DOG FRIENDLINESS Must be kept on lead near livestock

PARKING Roadside parking near Wedgwood visitor centre entrance

PUBLIC TOILETS Wedgwood visitor centre (customers only)

NOTES The canal tow path between Point ❸ and The Plume of Feathers is closed until November 2013. Either continue down the road through Barlaston from Point ❷ to join the tow path at the pub, or at Point ❸ stay on the track to the road and turn right along the pavement into Barlaston

During the 18th and 19th centuries white stoneware was all the rage, thanks in part to an influx of expensive white china from the Orient. In the quest for a cheaper alternative, potters experimented with powdered flint, which, when mixed with clay, helps to whiten it, but there were so many problems with the process that for a time English china was more expensive than silver. In the 1760s, Josiah Wedgwood perfected creamware and a few years later, when Queen Charlotte purchased an entire tea set, Josiah cannily changed the name to Queen's Ware.

JOSIAH WEDGWOOD

The Wedgwood family came from Burslem, now part of Stoke-on-Trent. Gilbert Wedgwood was recorded as the first Master Potter in the family in 1640, and his most famous descendant, Josiah, was born in 1730. Josiah worked in his father's pottery from the age of nine, and in 1744 he was apprenticed to his older brother Thomas.

BROKE THE MOULD

After a number of partnerships Josiah set up his own pottery in Burslem in 1759. Until then pottery had been something of a cottage industry, but Wedgwood broke the mould, building – for the first time ever – a pottery factory. Rather than rely on family members, he paid people to work in the factory, with materials and tools he supplied. This made the whole production process much more efficient and more lucrative.

A decade later, with business booming, Josiah built a bigger factory in Burslem which he called Etruria (at the time, Greek vases were believed to be Etruscan in origin). This became a model for other pottery manufacturers. Here he applied rigorous, scientific techniques to producing new, innovative pottery. The results of his efforts can still be purchased today and include Jasperware (characterised by unglazed, pale blue stoneware with white relief portraits or classical scenes) and black basalt ware, or Egyptian ware, a hard stone-like material used for vases and busts of historical figures. When Josiah died in 1795 his legacy wasn't just limited to porcelain. His success, vision and business practices made him a leading figure of the Industrial Revolution and his impact on the local countryside was immense, not least because of the canals that he was, at least in part, responsible for.

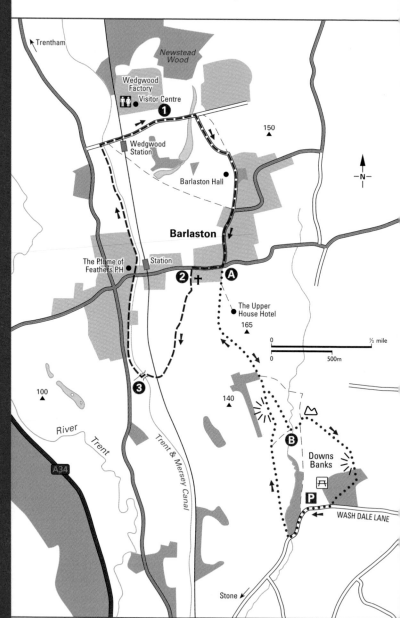

❶ From the visitor centre drive, head left across the lake and then right up the drive towards Barlaston Hall. Go past this hall and continue along the metalled road as far as the crossroads in Barlaston. At the crossroads turn right and after 250yds (229m), just past the Church of St John the Baptist on your left, head left along a wide gravel track.

❷ The track passes through a broad expanse of open farmland, with sweeping (if not altogether dramatic) views of the Trent and Mersey Canal to the right. After about 800yds (732m), before the third gate, go right on a less obvious but waymarked path around the edge of the field to reach a stile. After crossing the stile head right along a wide track, then cross the railway via an underpass, before bearing right to a bridge over the canal. Go over the bridge and take the steps down to the left.

❸ At the bottom of the steps head left and then follow the canal all the way to the first bridge (at Barlaston) and then the second (at Wedgwood Station). Head left here, up to the metalled road, and then right, back towards the visitor centre.

WHERE TO EAT AND DRINK The Plume of Feathers pub by Barlaston Station is a modern pub that offers a wide-ranging menu, including morning coffee and all-day bar food at weekends. The restaurant at the Wedgwood visitor centre also has a variety of light snacks and meals, as well as elegant afternoon tea – all served on Wedgwood fine bone china, of course.

WHAT TO SEE The Trent and Mersey Canal, completed in 1777, linked the River Trent at Derwent Mouth near Derby with the Bridgewater Canal at Preston Brook, near the mouth of the River Mersey. This effectively meant the country could be navigated all the way from the west coast to the east, and that fine clay from the West Country could be shipped to the doorstep of Wedgwood's factories. James Brindley designed and built both the Bridgewater and the Trent and Mersey, the latter comprising some 93 miles (150km) of waterway and 76 locks, not to mention a tunnel almost 1.75 miles (2.8km) long beneath the heart of Stoke-on-Trent.

WHILE YOU'RE THERE The Wedgwood Story visitor centre is a multi-million pound attraction featuring a museum, shop, two restaurants and, of course, the Wedgwood factory itself. As well as a fine display of rare and valuable exhibits, the museum also traces the rich history of the Wedgwood company and visitors can walk the factory floor to see the production process, from throwing to firing. You can take your turn at the potter's wheel, try your painting skills or talk to Wedgwood's craftspeople in the demonstration area. If you still have any energy for shopping, take time to browse for souvenirs, ornaments and tableware, including some exclusive lines. The centre is open year-round (except Christmas week and New Year's Day), Monday to Friday 10–5, weekends 10–4.

Downs Banks

DISTANCE 3.5 miles (5.7km)   **MINIMUM TIME** 1hr 30min

ASCENT/GRADIENT 656ft (200m) ▲▲▲   **LEVEL OF DIFFICULTY** ✚✚✚

SEE MAP AND INFORMATION PANEL FOR WALK 28

Leave the main route at the crossroads, Point **Ⓐ**, and go straight across, following signs to The Upper House Hotel. After 100yds (91m) stay straight along a track, ignoring the metalled road up to the hotel to your left. Continue along the bottom of the field as far as the swing gate and then head diagonally left across the next field, following an obvious dirt path.

At the far side of this field carry on above the next field, until you reach the edge of Downs Banks. Go through a gate and make your way along the top of the wide ridge for 100yds (91m) and fork left at a bridleway marker down a track to a stream. A little further on, cross the stream on the stepping stones to reach a path junction. Go second left (not hard left) through a gate, Point **Ⓑ**. Head left

and then, after 100yds (91m), go hard right up the steep spur of the hill.

Follow this trail all the way to the viewfinder at the top, and then continue along the top of the eastern bank until 50yds (46m) beyond a gate it forks right and drops steadily back down to a gate and Wash Dale Lane. At the road turn right, following it round to the left to a small footbridge by a ford. Head immediately right, back into Downs Banks and, after 150yds (137m), go left up a stepped track to the top, leaving the stream behind.

Walk along the top until you leave the woods behind. When you get to a fence ahead of you, go left through the gate and retrace your steps to rejoin the main route, at Point **Ⓐ**.

WHAT TO SEE Downs Banks were once crossed by an ancient packhorse trail from the East Midlands to Chester. They remained common land until the end of the 18th century, when they were enclosed by hedges for farming, traces of which can still be seen, particularly near the picnic sites. The land was used to grow hops bound for the nearby Joules brewery. In 1950, when the area was threatened with industrialisation from Meaford Power Station, 160 acres (65ha) were purchased by John Joules & Sons, endowed by public subscription and given to the National Trust. Today, a memorial stone of Cornish granite stands near the south corner of the park to commemorate this presentation, and to serve as a tribute to those who lost their lives during World War II.

Around Tutbury

DISTANCE 2.75 miles (4.4km)	**MINIMUM TIME** 1hr

ASCENT/GRADIENT 88ft (27m) ▲▲▲　　**LEVEL OF DIFFICULTY** ✚✚✚

PATHS Road and field track, many stiles

LANDSCAPE Town, farmland and riverside

SUGGESTED MAP OS Explorer 245 The National Forest

START/FINISH Grid reference: SK213294

DOG FRIENDLINESS Keep on lead at all times

PARKING Tutbury Mill picnic site

PUBLIC TOILETS At town car park in Tutbury

Tutbury boasts a long history of making – and finding – money, and nowhere is this more obvious than at the picnic site near the start of the walk. In 1781, a five-storey mill was built here on the Mill Fleam, an artificial braid of the River Dove. Originally it was a cotton mill employing more than 300 workers, with two 14ft (4.3m) waterwheels powering an astonishing 7,000 spindles. Mill Farm, across the road, was originally a warehouse.

PRODUCTION OF PLASTER

After more than 100 years the cotton mill closed, but in 1890 Henry Newton acquired it for making plaster of Paris from gypsum, mined in the Fauld Hills, west of Tutbury. In its purest form, gypsum is known as alabaster, and is ideal for ornamental carving. Gypsum is also used for brewing pale ale, which accounts for the flourishing beer industry in Burton upon Trent, 5 miles (8km) south. Production of plaster continued until 1968, when the mill was demolished, but British Gypsum still mines in the Fauld Hills.

A REMARKABLE FIND

Despite all this hard work and industry over the centuries, there were easier ways to find your fortune in Tutbury. In 1831, men excavating the river to improve the flow of water to the mill found several hundred medieval coins. The river was quarantined to prevent looting and a major dig was conducted. Remarkably, more than 100,000 silver coins were recovered, some of which can still be seen at the Stoke city museum in Hanley. The question was, where had the cash come from? The answer lay in a battle fought and lost over 500 years before by Thomas, Duke of Lancaster and Lord of Tutbury Castle. Thomas sided with the Scots against his cousin Edward II in the early 1300s, so the King attacked the castle to teach him a lesson. Thomas lay in wait at Burton Bridge, but was outflanked and duly defeated by Edward in 1322. His fortune was smuggled out of the castle, but the horses floundered crossing the river. When it was found in 1831, it was claimed by the Crown.

These days Tutbury is known more for its fine Georgian crystal than its bloody medieval heritage. The first glassworks were founded at the height of the Industrial Revolution, and today there are two in the village, both with excellent factory shops.

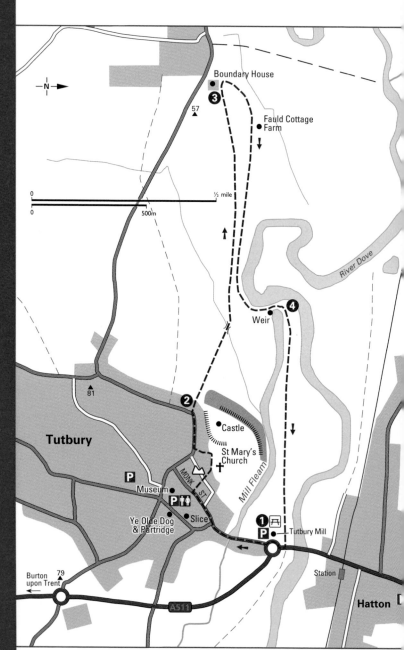

1 From the picnic site, head right at the roundabout into the town. Stay right at the first fork onto Monk Street and, after 150yds (137m), head right at Castle Court up a footpath to St Mary's Church. Pass the church and the castle entrance to reach the main road. Go right here and, at the top of a short hill, follow the footpath signs to the right.

2 Go down this footpath, veering half right onto the flood plain. In the far corner of the field go through the open gateway to the next and cross the stile a few paces away on the left. Head diagonally right to another obvious stile-footbridge-stile. Cut off the left corner of the field, aiming for the middle of the left-hand hedge. Cross the stile here and walk straight across the long meadow, heading for the left of some farmhouses in the distance. After 600yds (549m), at the meeting of two hedges, cross a double stile and continue with a hedge to your left. Cross another double stile at the end of this field and keep following the hedge to your left.

3 As you reach Boundary House, to your left, go right along the obvious concrete track back towards Fauld Cottage Farm. Head to the right of the farm gate, off the concrete, to a stile. Over the stile, head straight across the middle of the field to an obvious gate on the far side. After the gate, head straight towards the castle, back the way you came. At the far left corner of the meadow, very close to the river, cross the stile and skirt left around the bank beneath a line of trees. Cross Mill Fleam to the weir.

4 Now head sharp right into an open meadow. Follow the faint path along Mill Fleam back to the picnic site and the car park on the far side.

WHERE TO EAT AND DRINK There are two good coffee shops on the High Street, No. 8 and Slice, both serving a variety of light snacks and cakes. For something a bit more substantial, Ye Olde Dog & Partridge boasts two good restaurants. It is also one of England's oldest coaching inns, dating from the 15th century.

WHAT TO SEE The elaborate west door of St Mary's Church in Tutbury, built c.1160, is a fine example of Norman craftsmanship and is believed to have been made from local alabaster.

WHILE YOU'RE THERE The vast earthworks of Tutbury Castle date from c.1070, but much of the stonework that exists today dates from the 15th century. Mary, Queen of Scots, was imprisoned here by Elizabeth I, and during the Civil War it was a Royalist stronghold, after which it was demolished by Cromwell's troops.

Hanbury and its Crater

DISTANCE 4.75 miles (7.7km)   MINIMUM TIME 2hrs

ASCENT/GRADIENT 240ft (73m) ▲▲▲   LEVEL OF DIFFICULTY ✦✦✦

PATHS Meadow tracks and bridleways, many stiles

LANDSCAPE Farmland and bomb crater

SUGGESTED MAP OS Explorer 245 The National Forest

START/FINISH Grid reference: SK171279

DOG FRIENDLINESS Must be kept on lead near livestock

PARKING St Werburgh's Church car park

PUBLIC TOILETS None on route

The history of Hanbury starts with the legend of St Werburgh. During the seventh century AD Werburgh, daughter of pagan King Wulfere of Mercia, founded nunneries at Repton, Trentham, Weedon and Hanbury, the latter believed to have been situated to the east of what is now St Werburgh's Church.

ST WERBURGH

Legend has it that when Werburgh died she was buried at Trentham, but her body was stolen back by the people of Hanbury and buried in a new shrine near the nunnery. As a result Hanbury became a major centre for Christianity. When the Danes invaded in AD 875, Werburgh's body was moved to Chester for safe keeping, and it was there, in the cathedral, that she was finally laid to rest.

A WARTIME TRAGEDY

Today Hanbury is known for a much more recent tragedy. At 11am on 27 November, 1944, the village witnessed the largest explosion caused by a conventional weapon in either World War; only the atomic bombs at Hiroshima and Nagasaki were bigger. In all, 70 people were killed in the blast, and 18 bodies were never recovered.

The reason for the explosion is unclear, although the site is hard to miss, marked as it is by a crater more than 0.25 miles (400m) across and 100yds (91m) deep. The area around Hanbury is rich in gypsum and alabaster and a number of exhausted mine shafts became convenient storage depots for high explosives during the war. RAF personnel and Italian prisoners of war dispatched this arsenal with heightening urgency as the Allied offensive in Europe got under way, and it's thought that carelessness, inexperience and cost-cutting all had a part to play on that fateful November morning. The first the villagers knew about it was a distant rumble before the explosion proper, which blackened

the sky as tens of thousands of tons of soil and rocks were blasted into the surrounding landscape. An entire farm, including its occupants and livestock, disappeared completely, and dozens of underground munitions workers – both British and Italian – were killed. A reservoir for the nearby plaster works burst its dam, unleashing 6 million gallons (27 million litres) of water, boulders, mud and trees onto the factory below, killing 27 workers. The explosion could be heard from London, and was recorded as an earth tremor as far away as Geneva.

Today, nature has healed the scars on the landscape as hawthorn, larch and silver birch have re-colonised the crater and surrounding area, providing a habitat for, among other things, a vast colony of rabbits. There's still a gypsum works to the north, below which is an extensive system of mines spread over 10 square miles (26sq km).

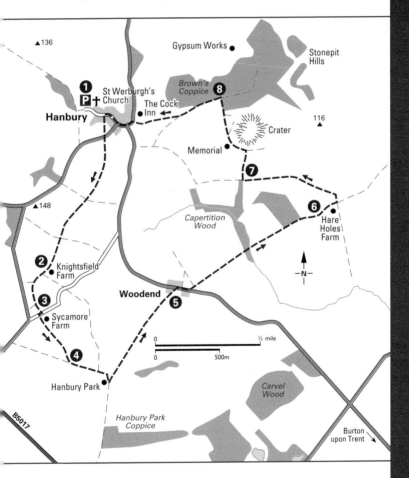

❶ From the car park, go back along Church Lane and after 150yds (137m), go right through a car park and a gate. Cross the field to a pair of stiles over a road and continue across the field to a gate, then to the corner of a hedge. Keeping this hedge to your right, head for Knightsfield Farm.

2 Go through the farm courtyard and along a rough surfaced track. As it bears to the right, follow a footpath sign, left, across stiles, keeping the hedge to your left. At a turning circle on a driveway go straight across to a footbridge before continuing, with the hedge to your left, to reach the road.

3 Turn right, then after 80yds (73m) go left at the footpath sign beside the building. Cross the yard into the field ahead to reach the stile at the bottom. Continue up the next field, crossing the stile at the top.

4 Where the hedge goes left, follow it across another stile and, via fields, aim for the imposing brick buildings of Hanbury Park. Go through a series of metal swing gates into the farm courtyard, then left past the open barn and through a wide gate away from the farm. Continue on the bridleway to Woodend.

5 At the road head right for 100yds (91m), then go left over a stile, making for a stile in the fence ahead and to the right. Head diagonally left across a field to a stile, then continue straight across the next field to a stile. Cross Capertition Wood to an open field, continuing with a hedge to the left, up a hill, across stiles, then down to another. At the end of the field cross one more.

6 Skirting to the left of the farm, climb over a series of stiles before turning sharp left immediately after an iron gate. Once across the stile in the corner, go ahead through three more fields, following waymarkers past a small pond. Drop down to the right-hand end of a bank of trees.

7 At a path junction turn right up a short hill via kissing gates, towards trees. Head round to the left to see the crater, now re-colonised by nature. Follow the path round to the left, past the memorial stone, to a bridleway leading away from it.

8 At the end of this bridleway, head left across a field, keeping the hedge to your right. Go through a kissing gate in the hedge ahead and continue straight ahead to a gate at the top. When you reach the end of the hedge on your left, go through a gate and a stile to return to Hanbury.

WHERE TO EAT AND DRINK The Cock Inn is a charming little pub with picnic tables and good views. It also has newspaper reports of the tragedy lining the walls for those who are interested in finding out more. It serves a wide variety of bar snacks and meals from Wednesday to Sunday, and is open all day at weekends and from 4.30pm Monday to Friday.

WHAT TO SEE The memorial just to the south of the crater is made of fine white granite, a gift from the Commandant of the Italian Air Force Supply Depot at Novara, in northwest Italy. The stone lists the names of the people killed, including those whose bodies were never recovered. It is a poignant reminder of the tragedy.

WHILE YOU'RE THERE Apart from the core of the west tower and the 13th-century arcades with round piers, St Werburgh's Church is of little interest architecturally, having been almost entirely rebuilt in the late 19th century. If the church is open (and it usually is), look for the window in the south aisle featuring a memorial to those who died in the explosion, made using fragments of 14th-century stained glass.

Stafford Castle

DISTANCE 4 miles (6.4km)   MINIMUM TIME 1hr 30min

ASCENT/GRADIENT 240ft (73m) ▲▲▲   LEVEL OF DIFFICULTY ✚✚✚

PATHS Pavement, gravel tracks and grass trails

LANDSCAPE Town, golf course, hilltop and farmland

SUGGESTED MAP OS Explorer 244 Cannock Chase

START/FINISH Grid reference: SJ918233

DOG FRIENDLINESS Keep on lead near livestock

PARKING Doxey Road pay-and-display at start; also at the castle

PUBLIC TOILETS Stafford Castle visitor centre and in town centre

In the 11th century, a castle was built on the hill to the west of Stafford by William the Conqueror to keep rebellious Saxons in check. It was at this time that the substantial earthworks you can see around the present-day castle were built. They involved a series of avenues, deep ditches, steep slopes and an impressive motte, or steep-sided earth mound, at the centre of the castle complex. Today, it's possible to take a tour of these earthworks by following a series of excellent information panels around the site.

HILLTOP HOME AND MILITARY HEADQUARTERS

Initially the site was more of a hilltop settlement, with wooden ramparts built in concentric rings behind a series of deep ditches. The castle proper would have been a three-storey timber keep on the motte, which doubled as the lord's residence and his military headquarters. The timber may have been plastered and painted to look like stone, to fool approaching enemies as well as to resist fire.

STONE CASTLE

It wasn't until the middle of the 14th century that Ralph, Lord Stafford, built the first stone castle on the site. It stayed in the family until 1521, when Henry VIII had Edward Stafford executed on a dubious charge of treason (he actually had a distant claim to the throne). The Staffords recovered their property and titles 25 years later but not their fortune. By the end of the 16th century the castle was in ruins, and remained so until the Civil War broke out in 1642. Isabel, Lady Stafford, was requested by Charles I to defend the castle against Parliamentary forces, and resisted months of siege. The castle continued to be neglected until Sir George Jerningham had the ruin cleared of debris in the early 19th century and rebuilt the eastern towers in an early example of Gothic revival architecture. The lords and ladies of the mid-19th century liked nothing better than to dress up their summer piles as Gothic follies complete with pointed arches and mock battlements.

Sir George never got around to the rest of the renovation. In 1961, a boy playing on the remaining stonework was killed by a collapsing window. The upper part of the building was demolished, although the council resisted calls to demolish the entire thing because it might still contain some of the original 14th-century masonry. Excavations begun in 1974 have confirmed this. The castle is preserved now, with a visitor centre providing a useful insight into the chronicle of the castle.

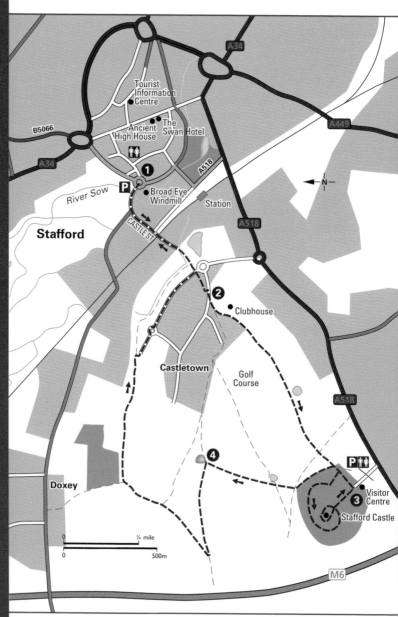

1 From the roundabout by Broad Eye Windmill head away from the town, over the river. After 100yds (91m) turn left along Castle Street, over the railway, and continue ahead on a cycle path to a roundabout. Cross and walk along the path, which soon joins the road on its left.

2 Cross over, turn right, then bear left by a line of trees, going left again at a footpath sign. Bear left here, keeping the houses to your right. Follow the gravel track up the middle of the golf course and, at the very top, keep going straight across the field ahead, following a faint grass path to the bottom left corner of the woods below the castle. A gap leads into the woods.

3 The path left leads to the visitor centre, but first keep up ahead for the castle's self-guided walk (0.75 miles/1.2km) following signboards in a spiral up to the stone keep. Descend the tarmac track to the visitor centre. This is packed with information on the Norman Conquest and features a short film on the history of the castle. There's also a shop selling snacks,

souvenirs and guides. From the visitor centre head uphill a few steps, then turn right on the wide path above the bottom of the wood to the gap (Point **3**), then skirt left around the outside of the wood. At the corner of the wood, go through a hedge and turn right down the field-edge path, with the hedge on your right. Descending through these fields serves to illustrate how tough it must have been for Saxon forces to charge in the opposite direction; even assuming they survived the onslaught of arrows from Norman longbows, by the time they got anywhere near the castle they'd have been absolutely spent.

4 At the foot of the field, with a pond just ahead, turn left above a tall ivy hedge, then cross a field. Cross a second field with a hedge on your left, then turn hard right on a wide track. Follow this downhill, then round to the right (you can use an old railbed alongside on the left here). When the track runs out, bear right onto a road and keep left across a roundabout. Just before the next roundabout head left on the cycle path, retracing your steps back into Stafford.

WHERE TO EAT AND DRINK There are numerous tea shops, bakeries, restaurants and bars to choose from in the town centre, from the exotic to traditional pub food, but you can't go wrong with The Swan, a former coaching inn dating from 1750 which features the original carriage entrance. The brasserie serves an extensive and varied menu, 12–10pm daily.

WHAT TO SEE Although the castle is barely 200ft (60m) higher than the surrounding countryside, it has surprisingly good views in every direction. From the top, looking out over the earthworks, it's easy to see how enemy forces could be spotted approaching from miles away, and how easy it must have been to defend.

WHILE YOU'RE THERE Built in 1595, Stafford's Ancient High House is today the largest timber-framed town house in England. Entry (free) Tue–Sat, 10am–4pm, throughout the year.

Shugborough Estate

DISTANCE 5.5 miles (8.8km)	**MINIMUM TIME** 2hrs 15min

ASCENT/GRADIENT 180ft (55m) ▲▲▲   **LEVEL OF DIFFICULTY** ✚✚✚

PATHS Gravel tracks, roads and tow paths

LANDSCAPE Forest, country park and canal

SUGGESTED MAP OS Explorer 244 Cannock Chase

START/FINISH Grid reference: SK004205

DOG FRIENDLINESS Must be kept on lead near main roads and in park

PARKING Seven Springs car park

PUBLIC TOILETS None on route

Shugborough, a 900-acre (365ha) estate on the edge of Cannock Chase, is without doubt the grandest stately home in Staffordshire. The ancestral pile of the Earls of Lichfield for more than 300 years, it was home to Thomas Patrick Anson, Fifth Earl of Lichfield, until his death in 2005. He was better known as the world-famous photographer Patrick Lichfield, second cousin to the Queen.

GRAND STATELY HOME

Originally built in 1693 as a small country manor, it has been altered and added to by successive generations of the Anson family, and by two people in particular: Thomas Anson (1695–1773) and his brother George (1697–1762). Thomas inherited the house in 1720, and made major changes over the next 50 years. The most significant alteration – or at least the one most apparent from the outside – was the addition of a magnificent eight-columned ionic portico designed by Samuel Wyatt in 1794. Much of this work was paid for out of George's own fortune: during his lifetime he had earned considerable fame and riches as a naval officer by capturing a Spanish treasure galleon. He later went on to become an admiral.

The house as we see it today is testimony to Thomas's ideals and what was considered the height of fashion for much of the 18th century. This was the age of reason, when industry and science were starting to take over the world; architects and their employers were keen to reflect this idea in their country piles, and the geometric simplicity of ancient Greek and Roman architecture seemed like a logical choice. It embodied the ideals of man being at the centre of the universe, taming nature with his new-found knowledge.

The gardens, too, were ordered and regimented, set out in a formal geometric pattern with the house at the centre of the estate. It was the same ideal that made classical motifs on Wedgwood pottery so enduring, and Thomas Anson was a patron of the famous potter.

Almost as a direct consequence of this insistence on law and order in gardens and architecture, the architects of the 19th century instigated a backlash against reason: romance was king, disorder was beauty, and the so-called 'Gothic' style enjoyed a revival in mansions and follies across England.

HELD IN TRUST

From the outside, the mansion today is much the same as it must have been during Thomas Anson's day. In 1966, following the death of the Fourth Earl of Lichfield, the estate was given to the National Trust. Since then it has been managed jointly by the Trust and Staffordshire County Council. The house isn't open all year, but the route of the walk can be completed at any time.

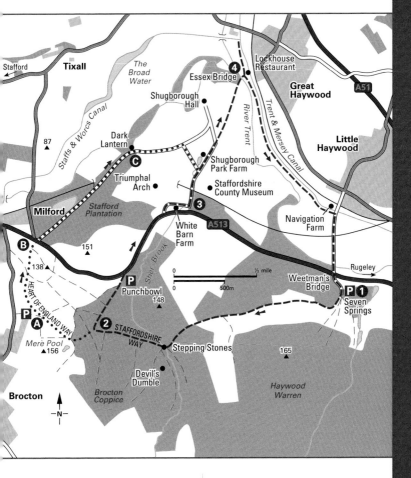

❶ At the end of the Seven Springs car park take the right-hand path, past a barrier, and at a junction in 130yds (119m) continue to the right.

Follow a gravel track, ignoring paths to the left or right, for 0.75 miles (1.2km) to Stepping Stones. Cross the stream here and turn right for 0.5 miles (800m) to reach a major T-junction.

2 Head right here, following the Staffordshire Way bridleway sign. Continue along a wide gravel track, again ignoring less obvious paths to the left or right, as far as the A513. Cross the road carefully and follow it right for 400yds (366m) before turning left at a road entrance to Shugborough Estate.

3 Follow the metalled road past the Staffordshire County Museum and the Hall's main car park and ticket office. Here you will also find the Craft Workshops and the Walled Garden. The garden was established in 1805 as a horticultural centre of excellence, and completely restored in 2007 to its original state (they are even growing historic varieties of fruit and vegetables that are quite rare today). Bear left to pass Shugborough Park Farm, then ignore the driveway bending left to the house itself, and instead keep ahead onto a tarmac bridleway. Take a look at the facade. From close range it's interesting to

note that the columns aren't made of stone at all, but are instead made of wood which has been clad with slate and painted to look like stone, a solution that would have been considerably cheaper. Follow the lane to the long, narrow Essex Bridge, and cross it to the canal beyond.

4 The route will continue along the tow path to the right; the Lockhouse Restaurant is just across the canal bridge ahead. By way of a short diversion, head under the canal bridge onto the tow path to the left. In just 350yds (320m) is the junction of the Trent and Mersey Canal with the Staffordshire and Worcestershire Canal. The toll-keeper's cottage has disappeared, but a toll house with arched windows and a kiosk still remain on the south side of the S & W. Return past the Lockhouse Restaurant and continue on the tow path (canal on your left) for a mile (1.6km). At Navigation Farm head right on the metalled road. Carry on over Weetman's Bridge, cross the A513 carefully, and continue up a short drive back to the car park.

WHERE TO EAT AND DRINK The Lockhouse Restaurant at Great Haywood is a convenient place to stop for a drink or a bite to eat. If the weather's warm, you can sit out by the canal and watch the world drift by; there's also a wide choice of hot meals, not to mention the biggest toasted teacakes you've ever seen. Open daily 10.30am–5pm throughout the year.

WHAT TO SEE There are no fewer than eight monuments of national importance in the parkland around Shugborough, but the most obvious of these en route are the Dark Lantern and the Triumphal Arch. These follies were designed by, among others, James 'Athenian' Stuart, a classicist whose popularity reflected the tastes of the time. Originally built by the Earl of Essex to gain access to Cannock Chase for hunting, the Essex Bridge is the longest packhorse bridge in England, and has never been widened.

WHILE YOU'RE THERE In addition to the house itself, the estate features a working farm museum in a second building designed by Samuel Wyatt, with demonstrations of farmhouse cooking, milking, and bread-, butter- and cheese-making by guides in period dress. The old servants' quarters, meanwhile, house the County Museum, where costumed actors recreate what life was like on the estate a hundred years ago.

Around Shugborough

DISTANCE 6.5 miles (10.4km)   MINIMUM TIME 2hrs 30min

ASCENT/GRADIENT 175ft (53m) ▲▲▲   LEVEL OF DIFFICULTY ✚✚✚

SEE MAP AND INFORMATION PANEL FOR WALK 33

At the track junction, Point ❷ of Walk 33, head left following the footpath sign to Mere Pool. When you reach the junction of a number of paths above the pool bear slightly left, now following a section of the Heart of England Way down a former railway cutting.

At the foot of the cutting, continue straight on, down the hill, shortly passing a pond and a house to your left. Go past the wooden barrier and through a long, narrow car park, Point ❹. At its far end veer right for a wide and well-used track.

Follow this up a slight hill onto a plateau and continue to another fork by a small pond. Bear slightly right here, following a fainter gravel path. Soon after you start to drop down the other side of the small plateau, you reach another fork of two dirt trails. Head right on the narrower and less-walked route and continue down through the woods, following the rim of a valley hollow down on your right. You reach the A513 opposite the main entrance of Shugborough Hall on the edge of Milford Common, Point ❸.

Take care when crossing the A513 and continue through the gates along a main driveway. Follow this for 1.25 miles (2km) through woodland to emerge into open parkland (Point ❻). To your left is the Dark Lantern building (also known as the Lanthorn of Demosthenes); on top of the hill to your right is the Triumphal Arch, or Arch of Hadrian. After 0.25 miles (400m), turn right on the tarmac estate road to the Hall's main car park. Walk through it and turn left, rejoining Walk 33 on the tarmac lane passing Shugborough Park Farm.

WHILE YOU'RE THERE If the house itself is open, it's well worth a visit as the interior is every bit as impressive as the exterior. In addition to a fine collection of 18th-century silver, paintings and furniture, the Lichfield Display Rooms give an insight into the photographic work of Patrick Lichfield, as well as featuring an unusual display of personal memorabilia, particularly with regard to George Anson's naval exploits. Josiah Wedgwood (see Walk 28) was a friend of the family, and a number of his pieces are included in the wide range of ceramics on display.

Shelmore Great Bank

DISTANCE 2.75 miles (4.4km)	**MINIMUM TIME** 1hr

ASCENT/GRADIENT 75ft (23m) ▲▲▲   **LEVEL OF DIFFICULTY** +++

PATHS Roads, dirt tracks and canal tow paths

LANDSCAPE Farmland, woodland and canal

SUGGESTED MAP OS Explorer 243 Market Drayton

START/FINISH Grid reference: SJ793229

DOG FRIENDLINESS Keep on lead on road

PARKING Roadside parking at Norbury Junction

PUBLIC TOILETS None on route

The Shropshire Union Canal, or 'Shroppie', runs 60 miles (96km) from the edge of Wolverhampton to the Mersey at Ellesmere Port, north of Chester. The canal is named after the Shropshire Union Railways and Canal Company, which was an amalgamation of a number of local canal companies.

WELSH RESIST RAILWAYS

The canal almost wasn't one. The intention was to build a railway using canal foundations, as it was believed that railways were a viable alternative to canals. However, Welsh resistance to railways meant that a canal was built instead using railway foundations, or, to be more precise, the foundations of railway engineering techniques. Instead of following a river, the canal took a direct route across country, through cuttings and on embankments, ostensibly to shorten journey times. The embankments in particular were major undertakings, as it was considerably harder to raise a wide watertight channel 60ft (18m) above the surroundings than it was to lay a railway line in the same way. One embankment on the Shroppie nearly scuppered the entire scheme – and it wasn't even necessary. Local landowner Lord Anson wanted to keep his wood unmolested for pheasant shooting, so he refused permission for the canal to pass through. The diversion involved building this vast embankment over a mile (1.6km) long and 60ft (18m) high.

THOMAS TELFORD

The man responsible for the embankment, and the rest of the canal, was Thomas Telford. Today he is remembered more as a bridge engineer than a canal builder, counting the Menai Suspension Bridge (then the longest in the world) among his many achievements. But the Shelmore Embankment caused him more than its fair share of problems. Even after moving millions of tons of earth from the cutting at nearby Woodseaves to build it, he had to cope with collapse after collapse. It took six years to build this embankment, and it was only made sound in 1835, a year after Telford's death.

SHROPPIE CHOCOLATE

The Shroppie remained in use until World War I. At the beginning of the 20th century, a chocolate maker called Mr Cadbury used it to pick up milk from farms between Norbury Junction and his chocolate factory at Knighton.

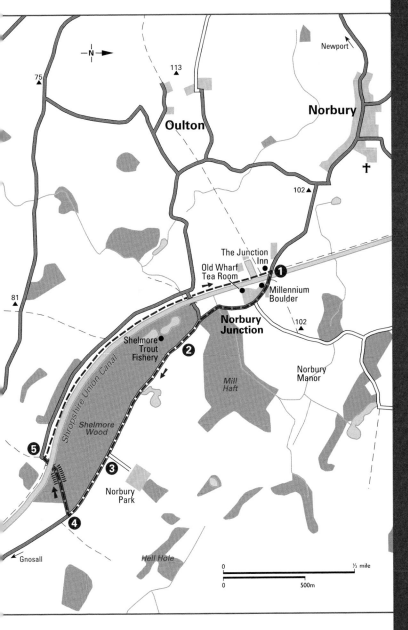

1 From The Junction Inn, follow the road towards Gnosall over the main canal and bear right, past the canal boat chandlers (and boat hire). On your right you pass one of the Norbury Boulders, originally transported by glacier from Scotland some 20,000 years ago, then the final 2 miles (3km) from nearby Gorse Farm rather more recently by low-loader. It's part of a linked walk past five boulders, the Norbury Millennium Boulder Trail. This one is the biggest, and shows dark 'xenoliths', fragments of the magma chamber wall incorporated into the granite as it solidified 400 million years ago. Continue to the point where the road heads sharp right under the canal, and go straight on up the wide gravel track that's signed for the Shelmore Trout Fishery.

2 When this track veers right into Shelmore Wood, keep going straight on along the edge of the wood, shortly coming to a gap in a high, tree-dotted hedge. Go through this gap onto an earth path with a line of conifers on the left masking a plantation of young oak trees, and the much older Shelmore Wood on your right. In spring and early summer, listen out for woodpeckers.

3 The path joins the concrete driveway from Norbury Park Farm on your left. Keep ahead, carrying on along the edge of Shelmore Wood as far as the Gnosall road. The cottage at the corner here shows a patchwork of stone and two ages of brickwork, the more regular patterning of the extension being less ancient than the main house.

4 Turn hard right on the road down a short hill. The cutting here shows the erosive power of people: the roadway has carved itself into the bedrock during the couple of millennia that people have been using it. At the bottom beware of cars as you walk through the tunnel (stop here and shout or sing: the acoustics are extraordinary).

5 Go through a gate on the left and up some steps to the canal. At the top turn left along the tow path. Follow the canal along its high embankment, finally crossing a brick arch over the disused side canal and back to The Junction Inn.

WHERE TO EAT AND DRINK The Junction Inn is a welcoming pub beside the marina. It offers bar snacks and main meals every lunchtime and evening and all day at weekends, when there's also a Sunday carvery. An outside hatch serves ice creams, and the beer garden overlooks the canal. On the opposite side of the canal is the Old Wharf Tea Room, open daily all year round for snacks and hot meals.

WHILE YOU'RE THERE At Norbury Wharf, opposite the pub, you can hire a narrowboat for a day's outing on the canal. There's also a gift shop where you can buy all manner of canal memorabilia. The Izaak Walton Cottage, 6 miles (9.7km) northeast, is also worth a visit. Walton was the author of *The Compleat Angler* (1653), the popular and enduring, fishing book (see Walk 17). The 17th-century cottage is now a museum to his life and work; it includes a first edition of his book. Free entry – call 01785 760278 for seasonal opening hours.

Abbots Bromley

DISTANCE 5.25 miles (8.4km)	MINIMUM TIME 2hrs
ASCENT/GRADIENT 525ft (160m) ▲▲▲	LEVEL OF DIFFICULTY ✛✛✛

PATHS Roads, grass trails and gravel tracks, many stiles

LANDSCAPE Farmland and village

SUGGESTED MAP OS Explorer 244 Cannock Chase

START/FINISH Grid reference: SK081245

DOG FRIENDLINESS Keep on lead at all times

PARKING Car park on Schoolhouse Lane, Abbots Bromley

PUBLIC TOILETS None on route

The existence of Abbots Bromley can be traced back to long before the Norman Conquest of England in 1066, through a number of references in charters and wills dating from that time. The first market charter was granted in 1221 for a weekly market and an annual two-day fair to be held in the village, and this fair survives today in the form of a rare and slightly unusual ritual. One theory on the obscure origins of the famous Horn Dance is that it derived from an ancient fertility rite, another is that the dance celebrates the establishment of ancient hunting rites.

AN OLD TRADITION

The Horn Dance was first performed at the Barthelmy Fair as long ago as 1226. This was originally held on the feast day of St Bartholomew, one of the Apostles and the patron saint of tanners, but an alteration to the Gregorian calendar in 1752 changed this date to 4 September. Today it's held on the first weekend after the 4th, with the dance proper taking place on the Monday.

DANCING ON THE VILLAGE GREEN

According to custom, six pairs of ancient reindeer horns (or more accurately antlers) are collected from St Nicholas's Church just before 8am by a small entourage of dancers comprising – among others – a fool, a hobby horse, a bowman and Maid Marion. The first dance of the day is performed on the village green with music provided by a melodion (a small reed organ similar to an accordion). Then a tour of the nearby villages, farms and pubs ensues with the final dance taking place back at the village green. In addition to the Horn Dance proper, this colourful procession also features displays of morris and clog dancing. Other attractions include exhibitions and craft stalls, plus the pleasures of no fewer than five pubs in Abbots Bromley alone. Each year the dance attracts hundreds of visitors from all over the world.

As well as the Horn Dance, Abbots Bromley is also linked to a number of other notable legends. The Goats Head pub was once patronised by infamous highwayman Dick Turpin, who is believed to have stayed the night there after stealing a horse from Rugeley Fair. And then there is the story of the Bagot goats: these black-necked beasts used to roam Bagot Woods to the north of the village and were first given to Sir John Bagot by Richard II at the end of the 14th century, in return for the hunting he enjoyed here. Legend has it that as long as the herd is maintained the Bagot family shall survive.

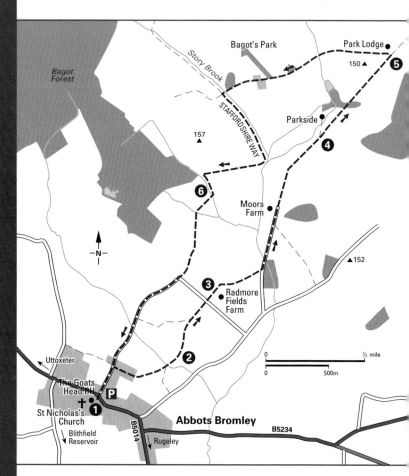

❶ From the wooden Buttercross, by The Goats Head pub, cross the road and go up Schoolhouse Lane. At the top of the hill turn right along Swan Lane, and when you get to the end head right along a path to a gate. Head diagonally left across the field to a gap in the hedge. Go through

this gap and continue across the next field to a footbridge. After crossing the footbridge keep following the faint grassy trail to a stile near the top right-hand corner of the field.

❷ Bear slightly left across the middle of the field to another stile. Carry on straight up the next field, keeping a hedge just to your left, across a series of stiles and fields, until you get to a road. Head straight across the road, following a footpath sign and, just as the track heads hard right, go straight on over a concrete stile and across the next field.

❸ After another stile, follow the curve of a field to the right as far as a metalled road. Go left here, following the road and track as far as Parkside farm gate. Just before this gate, go through a gate on the right, and then left through another series of gates.

❹ Continue across the field, with a hedge to your left, before crossing a funnel-shaped section of meadow to the small wood on the far side. Follow the path diagonally right through this band of trees to a pair of footbridges and another stile. Leaving the wood behind, head for the far right-hand corner of the field.

❺ At the road opposite Park Lodge turn left. Just after crossing Story Brook head left. At the far left-hand corner of the field, follow the hedge round to the right and cross a small copse. Continue to follow the fence towards the corner of Bagot Forest and then go left, through the hedge. With the hedge now on your right, walk around the edge of the field, swinging left, to go through another clear gap in the hedge.

❻ With Bagot Forest to your right, follow the Staffordshire Way footpath signs across the wide field ahead, aiming for the bottom end of a sloping hedge. When you reach it turn left and follow its right side up to a gate at the top of the field. Carry on straight along the track as far as a metalled road. Go straight on to get back to the start.

WHERE TO EAT AND DRINK There are five different pubs to choose from in Abbots Bromley, which is impressive for a large village. The Goats Head is arguably as friendly and welcoming as any, with timber beams throughout and excellent food served lunchtimes and evenings on weekdays and all day at weekends. Bar snacks and a variety of traditional hot meals are available.

WHAT TO SEE The wooden Buttercross (opposite The Goats Head pub and named after the produce once sold under it) would have been at the heart of the once thriving market and is thought to have been built in 1339. However, architectural historian Nikolaus Pevsner, in *The Buildings of England, Staffordshire*, gives a more likely date of the 17th century.

WHILE YOU'RE THERE Blithfield Reservoir, just to the west of Abbots Bromley, has been designated a Site of Special Scientific Interest (SSSI) thanks to the significant part it plays as a refuge for wildfowl and waders such as yellow wagtails, Canada geese, great crested grebes and herons. The shoreline at the north end of the causeway makes a very pleasant spot for a picnic, and in the summer there is often a takeaway food outlet selling snacks, hot and cold drinks and ice creams.

Rugeley and Colton

DISTANCE 3.5 miles (5.7km)	**MINIMUM TIME** 1hr 30min

ASCENT/GRADIENT 180ft (55m) ▲▲▲   **LEVEL OF DIFFICULTY** ✚✚✚

PATHS Roads, grass trails, tow path and gravel tracks, several stiles

LANDSCAPE Farmland, hilltop and canal

SUGGESTED MAP OS Explorer 244 Cannock Chase

START/FINISH Grid reference: SK045185

DOG FRIENDLINESS Keep on lead near livestock

PARKING Side-street parking near St Augustine's Church, Rugeley

PUBLIC TOILETS None on route

NOTES Fields near Point ❷ are sometimes grazed by a bull with cows; see alternative route

Although Rugeley can be traced back as far as Saxon times, today there's little evidence of the town's medieval past apart from the ruins of St Augustine's Church, built in the 12th and 13th centuries. When it needed rebuilding in the 19th century, the decision was taken to choose a new site and leave the original to the elements, with the result that the parish had two churches for the price of one.

MYSTERIOUS DEATHS

Apparently, though, no amount of building to the glory of God could deliver one local character from a life of infamy. Doctor William Palmer, the son of a timber merchant, married Ann Brooks in 1847. She subsequently bore him five children, but four died mysteriously in infancy. Ann's father also died under suspicious circumstances and, when her grieving mother came to stay, she too was dead within the space of a week. Later, when William owed money to a bookmaker, the bookie suddenly became very ill and died before he had a chance to collect his cash. In the meantime, William took out insurance policies for his wife and brother, but they both died soon after the first payments had been made. The insurance company refused to pay out, so – heavily in debt – William went to the races with a friend by the name of John Parsons Cook. As luck would have it, Cook won, but unfortunately died before picking up his winnings. So who do you suppose showed up to collect them? Why, Dr William Palmer of course!

MURDER MOST FOUL

By this stage, it wasn't just the insurance company who were crying foul, and Palmer was arrested for Cook's murder. The newspapers of the time called it the 'Trial of the Century' and for weeks it was headline news. After over a month in court Palmer was eventually found guilty and was publicly executed in Stafford at 8am on Saturday 14 June, 1856, in front of a crowd of 10,000. But that wasn't the end of William Palmer. So notorious were his crimes, and so voracious was the press in reporting them, that he endured for more than 100 years as a waxwork model in Madame Tussaud's Chamber of Horrors. Remarkably, it stayed there until 1979.

One story tells how the people of Rugeley were so horrified by the scandal surrounding the trial that they petitioned Parliament to change the name of the town. The Prime Minister considered the petition and agreed the town name could be changed, but only if they named it after him; the problem was, his name was Palmerston.

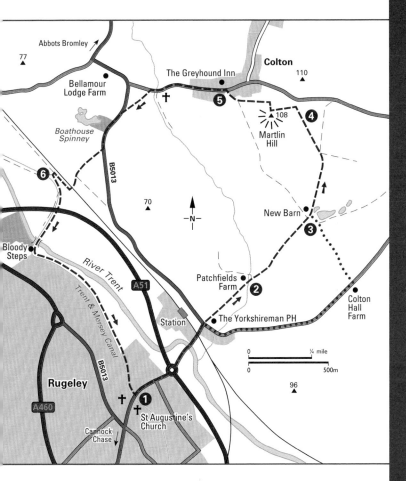

❶ From St Augustine's Church head right along the B5013 towards Abbots Bromley. After going over two roundabouts, the river and under the railway, continue straight on along the track just to the left of The

Yorkshireman pub. When you get to Parchfields Farm, go over a stile on the right and across a field to a pair of stiles and a footbridge. (Note: if you don't want to brave the bull that is sometimes in this field – he's fairly placid – then at The Yorkshireman turn right along Blithbury Road. After 0.5 miles (800m), opposite the entrance to Colton Hall Farm, turn left along a stony track to New Barn, Point ❸).

❷ Cross the footbridge and head diagonally left across the field to its far corner. Head over a stile here and straight along the right-hand edge of the field, keeping the hedge just to your right. At the end of the field, follow the yellow footpath arrows right and then left and continue in the same direction on a field track to meet the access track of New Barn.

❸ Turn left, passing to the right of the house onto a green track. Pass a pool, bearing slightly right, along the edge of the field, keeping the hedge to your right-hand side. The hedge curves round to the left and, after a further 220yds (201m), go through the gate in the top right-hand corner of the field. Continue in the same direction, again keeping the hedge to the right, until you get to the top of this field.

❹ Go through a gate and turn left behind a big shed for about 100yds (91m) to cross a stile on your right. Turn left alongside this fence, up to the top of Martlin Hill. At the summit turn 90 degrees to the right and follow the fence down to a stile on the left. Go over and head downhill to a stile in the bottom right corner. Join the short track ahead, which becomes Martlin Lane, into Colton.

❺ Turn left and walk all the way through the village. Just after a small bridge, as the road bends right, bear left onto a footpath. Head straight out across the field on a faint path. Follow this footpath until it brings you out onto the B5013 and then go left for 150yds (137m). Just after the road bends left, turn right, down a wide gravel track which crosses over the railway line before turning hard right for another 150yds (137m), to reach the canal.

❻ Without crossing the bridge, head left along the canal tow path and follow this all the way to the B5013. Just before you reach the bridge go up a ramp and then right, back to the start.

WHERE TO EAT AND DRINK The Greyhound Inn in Colton is a friendly and charming pub, serving a range of snacks and traditional main meals most evenings and at Sunday lunchtimes. It's open 5.30–11pm every weekday and from noon at weekends.

WHAT TO SEE Just after the canal crosses the river towards the end of the walk, you see the tow path on the far side of the canal leading to some steps. These steps were the scene of another infamous crime, when a woman named Christina Collins was murdered by three men in 1839. When they were caught, one was hanged, one was deported to Australia and the third was sent to prison. Christina's body was buried at the new St Augustine's Church.

WHILE YOU'RE THERE Nearby Cannock Chase offers some of the best mountain biking in the Midlands. With miles of wide gravel track and lots of free parking, it's ideal for both a short potter and an all-day epic. There's a bike centre and hire shop at Birches Valley Visitors' Centre, just west of Rugeley (see walks 38–40).

Cannock Chase and Springslade Lodge

DISTANCE 4 miles (6.4km)	MINIMUM TIME 1hr 30min	
ASCENT/GRADIENT 361ft (110m) ▲▲▲	LEVEL OF DIFFICULTY ✦✦✦	
PATHS Gravel tracks, dirt paths and roads		
LANDSCAPE Heather and woodland		
SUGGESTED MAP OS Explorer 244 Cannock Chase		
START/FINISH Grid reference: SJ980181		
DOG FRIENDLINESS Beware of cyclists at all times		
PARKING Ample parking at start point		
PUBLIC TOILETS None on route		

At the beginning of the 20th century Cannock Chase was very different from the way it is now, due to centuries of deforestation. A long history of iron smelting and the consequent demand for charcoal and then coal had left the landscape almost treeless.

ARMY TRAINING CAMP

The bleak landscape reflected bleaker times. With the outbreak of World War I, the Chase was the perfect place for an army training camp and, between 1914 and 1918, 250,000 British and Commonwealth troops passed through on their way to the trenches. Many would not return.

The camp occupied much of the area of this walk. There were training areas and firing ranges, a railway, sewage works, prisoner of war camp, powerhouse and pumping station, and quarters for troops and officers. Also important were the veterinary hospital at Chase Road Corner and the Great War Hospital at Brindley Heath, for wounded soldiers brought back from the front. Many German, British and Commonwealth soldiers who died in the War Hospital were buried in the Commonwealth Cemetery, now a quiet, contemplative, immaculately preserved place. Equally moving is the German War Cemetery, to the northeast. It was established by the German War Graves Commission, which was asked by the German government to take care of over 1.4 million graves, in 343 cemeteries throughout 24 different countries.

After the German-British War Graves Treaty of 1959, most of the German soldiers in cemeteries around Britain were exhumed and transferred to the cemetery at Cannock Chase, and today it is the only German war cemetery in the UK. It is the final resting place for 2,143 servicemen who died in World War I and 2,797 who died in World War II. In all, 1,307 Germans remain in other British cemeteries (including the Commonwealth Cemetery here).

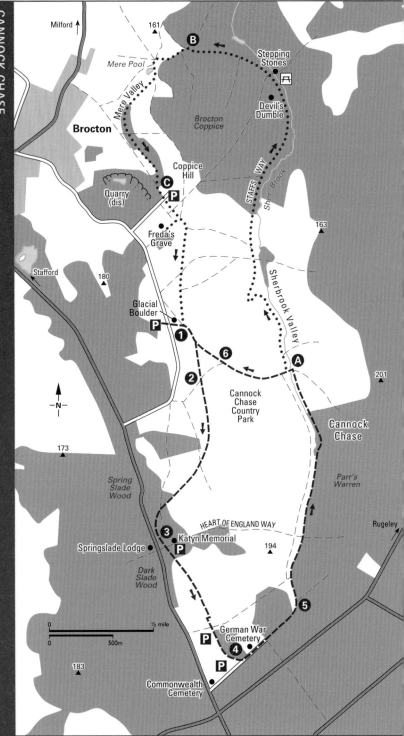

Milford ↑

161 ▲

B

Stepping
Stones

Mere Pool

Mere Valley

Devil's
Dumble

*Brocton
Coppice*

Brocton

Coppice
Hill

C

P

Quarry
(dis)

STAFFS WAY

Sher Brook

163 ▲

Freda's
Grave

Stafford

180 ▲

Sherbrook Valley

Glacial
Boulder

P

1

6

A

201 ▲

2

Cannock
Chase
Country
Park

**Cannock
Chase**

173 ▲

*Spring
Slade
Wood*

*Parr's
Warren*

Rugeley

HEART OF ENGLAND WAY

3 Katyn Memorial

Springslade Lodge ●

P

194 ▲

*Dark
Slade
Wood*

5

0   ½ mile

0   500m

183 ▲

P German War
Cemetery

4

P

Commonwealth
Cemetery

—N—

1 From the Glacial Boulder, walk away from the road along a narrow path past the trig point. Turn right along the wide gravel track. When you get to a fork, go right, following the Heart of England Way footpath sign.

2 At a crossroads of paths, keep ahead (ignoring a footpath to the right). At the next path junction, again carry straight on as the path curves gradually around the right. Continue along this track across several more path crossroads until your path enters trees and curves round to the left alongside the road. Where another wide track comes in from the left, go straight on rather than taking the shortcut down to the road on the right. Soon you meet the narrow surfaced road opposite Springslade Lodge. (The Katyn Memorial is just up to the left here.)

3 Cross the side road, and walk up a dirt track and across a path crossroads. After about 500yds (457m) you come to a T-junction which requires a dog-leg right, then left, to keep going in the same direction and across the end of a car park. Continue

in this direction to a second car park and, as the track curves around to the left, another metalled road.

4 Turn left past the German War Cemetery. In 100yds (91m) the road becomes a wide gravel track. Continue for another 0.25 miles (400m) down into the woods, and when you get to the fork go left down into the head of Sherbrook Valley.

5 Continue along the bottom of the valley for a mile (1.6km), staying to the right of the stream and ignoring all paths off, to a track junction with a ford down on the left. Cross the stream on the stepping stones. At the junction on the other side, head away from the stream following a stony track slightly left around the bottom of a hill ahead, rather than a path slightly right, straight over the top of it. Follow this track as it curves round to the right, up onto the plateau.

6 Continue across the plateau until the path starts to descend the other side, at which point you rejoin your original path, heading right, back to the Glacial Boulder and car park.

WHERE TO EAT AND DRINK Springslade Lodge is a great place to stop for refreshments in the summer, with plenty of outside seating, but its indoor tea room is also popular in the winter (currently open daily, even in winter). It offers hot snacks and tasty main meals.

WHAT TO SEE To the right of the German Cemetery building are the massive grave stones for four Zeppelin crews shot down over England in World War I. They were originally buried in Potters Bar, Burstead and Theberton. Much harder to find are the graves of the 90 unknown soldiers; one near the centre is marked simply: 'Zwei unbekannte Deutsche Soldaten.'

WHILE YOU'RE THERE The Katyn Memorial, near Springslade Lodge, is a tribute to the 14,000 members of the Polish armed forces and professional classes executed in 1940 in Katyn Forest, near Smolensk, by the Soviet secret police on the orders of Stalin. The Poles had been prisoners of war following the Soviet Union's invasion of Poland while Germany was invading from the west.

Coppice Hill and Freda's Grave

DISTANCE 7 miles (11.3km)   MINIMUM TIME 2hrs 30min

ASCENT/GRADIENT 361ft (110m) ▲▲▲   LEVEL OF DIFFICULTY ✦✦✦

SEE MAP AND INFORMATION PANEL FOR WALK 38

After crossing the stream at the ford with stepping stones, Point **Ⓐ**, turn to the right along the Sherbrook Valley, on the wide, sandy path to the left of the stream. In 550yds (500m) it veers left, but soon turns sharply back to rejoin the stream; it's now signed 'Staffordshire Way'. Continue along the stream to pass the picnic site on the other side of Stepping Stones. Don't cross the stream, but carry on past the ford and stepping stones for 0.25 miles (400m) to a T-junction in the tracks, Point **Ⓑ**. Turn left here, leaving the Staffordshire Way, and follow a sign for Mere Pool.

At the next major path junction, above Mere Pool, turn hard left almost back on yourself, following signs for the Heart of England Way towards Coppice Hill. Carry on along the bed of the old camp railway, gradually rising up the side of Mere Valley, ignoring any paths off to the left or right. The track bends up left into the small side valley, Hollywood Slade. At its top, Point **Ⓒ**, bear slightly left to cross a metalled road and then continue in the same direction as before.

After 150yds (137m) turn right on a grass path, soon with a signpost 'FG' pointing to Freda's Grave 100yds (91m) on down the path. Return to the main path, turning right. Continue along it for 80yds (73m), then take the right fork, still following the Heart of England Way. Go across the next diagonal crosspaths and continue the final 400yds (366m) to turn off right to the trig point and Glacial Boulder at the walk start.

WHAT TO SEE The area around Mere Pool used to be the camp sewage works and sludge beds. The path along the side of Mere Valley beyond the pool was a part of the camp railway which connected with the station in Milford a mile (1.6km) or so to the north. The Glacial Boulder stands on the base of what was once the camp reservoir tower. The boulder itself is Criffel granite, originating in southwest Scotland. It fell onto a southbound glacier during the last ice age and was deposited near by when the ice melted.

WHILE YOU'RE THERE Freda, canine mascot of the New Zealand Rifle Brigade, was a Dalmatian adopted by the brigade when they were camped at Cannock Chase, and it's thought that she accompanied them to the Battle of the Somme in 1916. Today, more than 70 New Zealand soldiers are buried at the Commonwealth Cemetery, while Freda was buried at Cannock Chase in 1918. Her collar, bearing the inscription 'Freda of the NZ Rifle Brigade', is kept in the Army Museum at Waiouru, New Zealand.

Cannock Chase

DISTANCE 3.5 miles (5.7km)	MINIMUM TIME 1hr 15min	
ASCENT/GRADIENT 270ft (82m) ▲▲▲	LEVEL OF DIFFICULTY ✚✚✚	
PATHS Gravel tracks		
LANDSCAPE Forest and forest pools		
SUGGESTED MAP OS Explorer 244 Cannock Chase		
START/FINISH Grid reference: SK018172		
DOG FRIENDLINESS Can be off lead, but beware of bikes		
PARKING Birches Valley Forest Centre pay car park		
PUBLIC TOILETS At Forest Centre at start		

Cannock Chase, a vast area of open heathland and conifer forest just to the north of Birmingham, has been the site of human activity for thousands of years. Prehistoric hunter-gatherers built massive earthworks here (see While You're There), and William the Conqueror, realising that the heavily forested area would be difficult to cultivate, declared it a royal hunting forest. As a result, anyone caught killing a small animal lost an eye or one hand, while anyone caught poaching deer was executed.

IRON RESOLVE

The precedent set by William I protected the Chase from being exploited for timber, and it remained a hunting forest until Tudor times. Under Henry VIII, however, the the Chase was given to William Paget, later the Marquis of Anglesey, who secured a licence to fell trees for iron smelting in 1560. Marquis's Drive, running more or less right across the chase, is a reminder of his legacy, but it was his deeds rather than his name that had the greatest impact on the landscape.

Iron smelting relied on vast quantities of charcoal to fire early blast furnaces. With the help of water-powered bellows, a mixture of charcoal, limestone and cinders was burned to melt the iron ore, which was then poured into troughs as cast iron, an alloy of carbon and iron. This mixture was very brittle, and even more charcoal was needed to burn off the carbon so that it could be hammered into wrought iron. The bars of iron produced in this way were then heated a final time, to be rolled flat and slit by a water-powered mill. By the end of the 16th century, the process was refined enough to produce items like nails, locks and chains. But the new technology came at a price, and by 1610 Cannock Chase had been almost completely deforested by voracious charcoal-burners.

CHASING COAL

It was still treeless 240 years later when the Cannock Chase Colliery came into being. The area was first mined for coal in 1298 but it wasn't until the height of the Industrial Revolution that it became big business. With coal came people, and the increase in population pushed back the boundaries of the remaining green areas further still.

THRILL OF THE CHASE

Mining continued well into the 20th century, and it wasn't until the 1920s and 1930s that trees began to be systematically replanted in the area. By the end of World War II, coal mining was confined to larger pits, and many of the smaller pits were closed. In 1958 much of the woodland and heather was declared an Area of Outstanding Natural Beauty (AONB), and since then most of it has returned to nature.

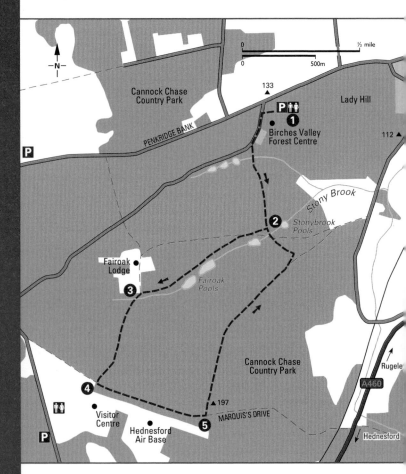

1 From the car park at the Birches Valley Forest Centre, turn left along the metalled road (Birches Valley) past a row of houses. After 200yds (183m), turn left along a wide gravel forest road. Stay left on the main track here, avoiding a less obvious grass track up the hill to the right. In 0.5 miles (800m) you reach a track junction just before Stony Brook.

2 Turn right, with a small sign for Cannock, along another smooth track. At once fork left, on a track along the valley floor. One of the small Stonybrook Pools is on your left; 300yds (274m) later you emerge into more open ground alongside two reservoirs, the Fairoak Pools. About 350yds (320m) after the second pool, you reach a major track junction.

3 Here turn left, following cycle signs for Cannock. In 100yds (91m) the main track bears right, ignoring smaller paths off to left and ahead. The path runs uphill, with clear-felled ground to the left and mature conifers to the right (these too may

soon be felled). Ignore lesser paths off left and right, and walk on to a junction at the top of the slope, beside a trail bikes signboard. Go straight across for another 150yds (137m) to meet a metalled, car-free road, Marquis's Drive.

4 Turn left along Marquis's Drive (or the bike path alongside). After 0.25 miles (400m) you pass the entrance to the disused air force base of Hednesford on your right. From this point Marquis's Drive becomes unsurfaced. It heads gently uphill and bends left. About 0.25 miles (400m) from the air base entrance, and just before the very top of the slope, a smaller track turns off left, with a blue bridleway arrow.

5 Turn left on this long, straight track, which dips downhill between the rows of conifers. At the bottom of the hill, turn left along a wider track, keeping ahead to Stony Brook. Cross the stream and continue ahead (Point **2**), retracing the route to the car park.

WHERE TO EAT AND DRINK The Birches Valley Café at the Forest Centre is open daily throughout the year and sells snacks and refreshments, including sandwiches, salads, jacket potatoes, soup and speciality coffees.

WHAT TO SEE Cannock Chase is home to five different species of deer: fallow, muntjac, red, roe and sitka. Spot the posts with reflective strips alongside the roads that cross the chase. The strips are set at an angle, so that when they're hit by the glare of car headlights, they bounce an arc of red light into the surrounding woods. Nearby deer are stopped in their tracks, preventing them from running into the path of the car.

WHILE YOU'RE THERE The Castle Ring, just a few miles southeast of the visitors' centre, dominates the highest point on Cannock Chase and offers impressive views. Enclosing an area of more than 14 acres (5.6ha), this vast earthwork comprises a triple rampart of steep banks and deep ditches, thought to have been built between 2,000 and 3,000 years ago as either a beacon or a fortress.

Historic Brewood

DISTANCE 5.75 miles (9.2km)	**MINIMUM TIME** 2hrs

ASCENT/GRADIENT 75ft (23m) ▲▲▲   **LEVEL OF DIFFICULTY** ✚✚✚

PATHS Tow paths, grass trails and roads

LANDSCAPE Canal, farmland and reservoir

SUGGESTED MAP OS Explorer 242 Telford, Ironbridge & The Wrekin

START/FINISH Grid reference: SJ881088

DOG FRIENDLINESS Must be kept on lead near livestock

PARKING Walkers eating at the Bridge Inn can use car park; street parking in Brewood

PUBLIC TOILETS Brewood village centre

Brewood is pronounced 'brood', and getting this right first time round will instantly endear you to locals. The name Breude in the Domesday Book (1086) is from the Celtic *bre*, or hill, and the Old English *wuda*, meaning wood.

ROMAN ROADS

It was during the Roman occupation of Britain that the line to the north of Brewood was established as a main transport route when Watling Street was built, from London all the way to present-day Wroxeter, just west of Shrewsbury. It was one of dozens of major roads built by the Romans across Britain, the longest of which were the Fosse Way (from Exeter to Lincoln), Ermine Street (from London to York) and Watling Street itself, built in the first years of the invasion (AD 100), and later extended to Chester.

BUILT TO LAST

Roman roads in Britain were an extension of a systematic network connecting Rome to the four corners of its vast empire, built principally as a means of moving its great armies quickly and efficiently across occupied countries. In order to do this the roads had to be exceptionally well constructed. They were usually built on a raised embankment (to allow adequate drainage), made out of rubble obtained from drainage ditches dug on either side. Next came a layer of sand, or gravel and sand, sometimes mixed with clay; and finally the whole thing was metalled with flint, finer gravel or even the slag from the smelting of iron. The finished road was often several feet thick, cambered to allow water to run off it and with kerb stones on each side to channel any excess water.

Left: Fairoak Pools, Cannock Chase at sunset (Walk 40)

Given the complexity of the roads, the huge distances covered and the realisation that every single inch was laboriously built by hand, the fact that many Roman roads – or at least their foundations – still exist today provides mute testimony to the mind-boggling efforts of their builders.

In addition to being well designed and well maintained, Roman roads almost invariably followed straight lines. Today's A5 follows the route of Watling Street for much of its length, and you only have to look at an atlas to see how much straighter it is than any modern road. This was achieved by lining up marker posts, and the result meant both faster journey times and a much more efficient communications network. It's worth noting that the Shropshire Union Canal, which bisects Watling Street to the north of Brewood, was built along similar principles, raised on great embankments and built in a series of straight lines, to improve travel times (see Walk 35).

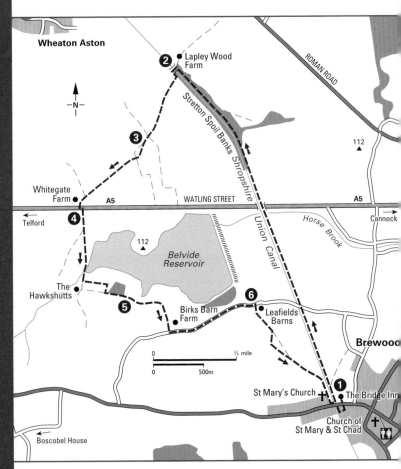

1 From The Bridge Inn car park, go straight across the main road and down some steps to the canal. Go right at the bottom of the steps and follow the canal tow path to pass over the A5 and then through Stretton Spoil Banks to Bridge No. 17 near Lapley Wood Farm.

2 Cross over the bridge and, at the concrete track, turn left for 100yds (91m). Just after this track bears right, go through the gate in the hedge to your right. Follow the hedge along the edge of the field and then along a dirt trail along a thin strip of woodland.

3 At the end of the trees, go through the gate directly ahead and then diagonally left across a field to its left-hand corner. Go through another small gate and keep ahead along the left-hand edge of the field. At the end of this very large field go through the gate and across another small field to the edge of Whitegate Farm. Skirt round the left-hand edge of the courtyard to reach a gate onto the A5.

4 Take care crossing this busy main road and then head left for 50yds (46m) before turning right along a metalled farm road. Follow this as far as The Hawkshutts. Opposite the corner of the garden wall, go left through a gate. Keep ahead to the right of the hedge, and then across a field, to pass along the right-hand edge of the wood ahead (the wood has a pond in it). Continue across the next field to a gate ahead.

5 After going through the gate, bear right along a path through bushes and trees and through the gate into another field. Bear slightly left here, aiming for a cottage with tall chimneys, until you get to a gate and a gravel-surfaced farm track. Turn right, along this track past Birks Barn Farm to a road. Turn left for 0.5 miles (800m), as far as Leafields Barns.

6 Go over a stile on the right, then after a second beyond a driveway go diagonally left across a field in the direction of the church steeples until you get to a stile. Cross the stile and head right, around the edge of the field, to a line of trees down the middle. Head left here, following the line of trees as far as a field track. Go ahead up the track to the canal and then turn right, back towards St Mary's Church and the start.

WHERE TO EAT AND DRINK The Bridge Inn is a warm and welcoming pub, pleasantly situated beside the canal. It serves a tasty and reasonably priced range of hot and cold snacks and main meals, available at lunchtimes and evenings daily, and 12–7pm on Sunday. Dogs and walkers are welcome.

WHAT TO SEE Colonel Carless, a Brewood soldier who fought alongside Charles II at the Battle of Worcester in 1651 and hid with him in the oak tree, is buried in Brewood Church cemetery. The church itself, dedicated to St Mary and St Chad, owes its surprising size to the fact that successive Bishops of Lichfield owned a medieval manor near Brewood.

WHILE YOU'RE THERE Boscobel House, 3 miles (4.8km) to the west of Brewood, played a part in the Civil War. Charles II, determined to reclaim the English throne when his father was executed on the orders of Parliament in 1649, fought the Parliamentary forces at Worcester two years later, but his army was routed. He fled and was forced to seek sanctuary at the hunting lodge of the royalist Giffard family, hiding himself in an oak tree there.

Around Lichfield

DISTANCE 2.5 miles (4km)   MINIMUM TIME 1hr

ASCENT/GRADIENT Negligible ▲▲▲   LEVEL OF DIFFICULTY ✚✚✚

PATHS Roads, surfaced paths and dirt trails

LANDSCAPE Town centre and parkland

SUGGESTED MAP OS Explorers 232 Nuneaton & Tamworth; 244 Cannock

START/FINISH Grid reference: SK118095

DOG FRIENDLINESS Must be kept on lead near roads

PARKING Debenhams multi-storey (442 spaces) near bus station

PUBLIC TOILETS Town centre locations and Beacon Park

The story of Lichfield begins soon after the death of Christ. In about AD 300, during the reign of Roman Emperor Diocletian, 1,000 Christians were martyred in this area. The name Lichfield, which means 'field of the dead', commemorates the event. As a martyr shrine, it soon became a centre of Christianity, and in AD 669 the first Bishop of Mercia, Chad, established his seat here. Although Chad only lived as a bishop for three years, such was his zeal and holiness that he converted many to Christianity.

GOTHIC CATHEDRAL

When Chad died in AD 672, he was buried close to the existing Church of St Mary. It wasn't long before his shrine became known as a place for miracles, and in AD 700 a new church dedicated to St Peter was built to receive his body. Later, a Norman cathedral was built on the same site, but a new Gothic cathedral was begun in 1085, this time dedicated to St Chad. Finally, after 150 years, the greatest cathedral in all the land was finished...

PLACE OF PILGRIMAGE

Imagine you're a peasant living near Lichfield when the cathedral is first completed. You have a small wattle and daub (wood and mud) house, some leather jerkins and sackcloth shoes. You might have seen a small Saxon or Norman church before, but if you live out in the country, you've probably never seen a stone building in your life, let alone one higher than two storeys.

SOARING SPIRES

You hear people talking about a new church being constructed in nearby Lichfield. They say it's built of stone and reaches up to the heavens, but nothing you've heard can prepare you for the sheer scale of what you find when you make your pilgrimage to this new house of God. Three gigantic spires soar into the sky and when you get close, approaching the vast west facade, it's so big that it feels as if it's falling on top of you.

GOLD AND SILVER

The cathedral as we see it today has hardly changed from the one exalted by Christian pilgrims and peasants 800 years ago. If anything, it was probably even more impressive in those times. Much of the stonework was painted silver and gold and the interior would have been more foreboding, lit only by the stained-glass windows of medieval times. Most of the stained glass in the cathedral today dates from the 19th century and is much lighter.

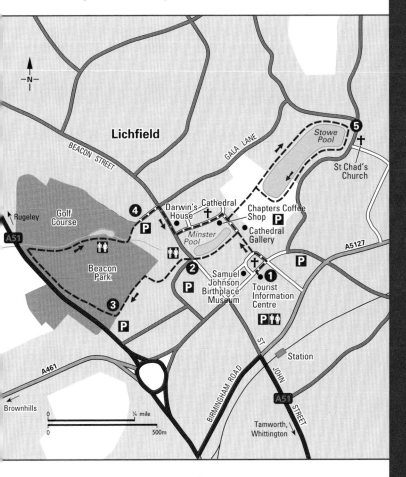

❶ From the tourist information centre, next to the Garrick Theatre, go through the Three Spires shopping arcade and turn left onto Conduit Street and ahead to Market Square. Walk straight along Dam Street, past a series of tea shops and cafes, until you get to Pool Walk. Go left here, keeping Minster Pool on your right-hand side, until you get to Beacon Street.

2 Go diagonally right over Beacon Street to the public toilets and the entrance to Beacon Park. Pass a fountain, and keep to the left of the bowling green and then the playing fields, on a path along the left edge of the park.

3 Pass through a car park and then bear right, following a tarmac cycle path to the far end of the playing fields. After the path has entered the narrow band of trees, and just before the A51, turn right along a gravel path and carry on to the golf course at the far end. Just before the footbridge onto the golf course, turn right and follow the small brook back along the edge of the playing fields until you reach a small lake. In the summer it's possible to hire boats here for a potter on the water. Continue past the lake before crossing a footbridge to the left to pass through a small car park into Shaw Lane.

4 Follow Shaw Lane to Beacon Street, turn right for 150yds (137m) and then left along The Close to reach the cathedral. If you're not in any rush, it's worth doing a quick circuit of the cathedral inside and out, before continuing. There's an excellent shop with leaflets and guides and a free leaflet is also available, which describes the cathedral's highlights. Bear to the right of the cathedral and, at the end of The Close, just after Chapters Coffee Shop, go right down Dam Street and then immediately left down Reeve Lane. Keep right on a hedged path ('no bikes') to Stowe Pool. From the far end of Stowe Pool you can look back at the cathedral's spires and see right through the windows from one side to the other, giving the impression that they're lighter and more delicate than stone.

5 Continue on the popular surfaced path all the way round the edge of Stowe Pool and return to Dam Street. Turn left past the end of Minster Pool to retrace your steps to the tourist information centre at the start.

WHERE TO EAT AND DRINK Chapters Coffee Shop is the ideal spot to stop for morning coffee, Sunday lunch or afternoon tea. It has a wide variety of snacks, meals and traditional English desserts, and a welcoming and relaxed setting right across from the cathedral.

WHAT TO SEE The Cathedral's chapter house boasts the Lichfield Gospels, an illuminated Latin manuscript from the eighth century. It's hard to imagine that the elaborately decorated pages of this ancient book were written, painted and bound more than 1,200 years ago. The Chapel of St Michael is where the campaigns of the Staffordshire Regiment are commemorated. It also has a book of remembrance with names of those who fell in the two World Wars.

WHILE YOU'RE THERE Lichfield is a pretty market town with great shopping and plenty to see. Among the highlights are the Samuel Johnson Birthplace Museum, commemorating the life and work of the celebrated writer who, along with a number of famous sayings, was responsible for the first comprehensive English dictionary. Also worth visiting is the house of Erasmus Darwin (1731–1802), the grandfather of Charles Darwin, who was a brilliant doctor, scientist, inventor and poet.

Right: Lichfield Cathedral from Pool Walk (Walk 42)

Around Whittington

DISTANCE 6.75 miles (10.9km)	**MINIMUM TIME** 2hrs 30min

ASCENT/GRADIENT 180ft (55m) ▲▲▲   **LEVEL OF DIFFICULTY** ✦✦✦

PATHS Roads, gravel and sand tracks, dirt trails, may be muddy after rain

LANDSCAPE Farmland and forest

SUGGESTED MAP OS Explorer 232 Nuneaton & Tamworth

START/FINISH Grid reference: SK158083

DOG FRIENDLINESS On lead near livestock and roads

PARKING Ample roadside parking in Whittington

PUBLIC TOILETS None on route

NOTES At time of checking (Feb 2013) the military firing range is in very occasional use (mostly on Sundays) – check for the red flag at the top of Hopwas Hays Lane before starting

Whittington Barracks, just south of the village of the same name, has been the home of the Staffordshire Regiment since 1881. The regiment dates back to 1705, when the 38th Foot was raised at the King's Head Hotel in Lichfield by Colonel Luke Lillingston, and it first saw active service fighting the French and Spanish in the West Indies. The raising of other regiments over the next 120 years eventually led to the formation of the Staffordshire Regiment after World War II, and its recent amalgamation into the Mercian Regiment. It was conferred the title of the Prince of Wales's in 1876. Today its Colonel in Chief is HRH the Duke of York, Prince Andrew. All of this history, and much more besides, is related by the Staffordshire Regiment Museum at Whittington Barracks. Perhaps the most interesting of the displays is the one dedicated to the story of those in the regiment who have been awarded the highest wartime honour.

ACTS OF VALOUR

The Victoria Cross was first established by royal warrant in 1856, to recognise acts of uncommon valour during the Crimean War, 1854–56. It was ordained that it should 'only be awarded for most conspicuous bravery, or some daring or pre-eminent act of valour or self-sacrifice or extreme devotion to duty in the presence of the enemy'. All VCs are forged from the remains of two Russian cannon, captured at Sebastopol, the last great battle of the Crimean War. The metal is guarded by 15 Regiment in Donnington, secured in vaults and rarely removed; the most recent issue of metal, sufficient to make 12 medals, was made in 1959. It's thought the remaining metal is enough to make a further 85 medals; given that only 14 have been won since the end of World War II, it can be expected that this will suffice for many years to come.

In all, 1,356 Victoria Crosses have been won, and of these, 1,156 were awarded before the end of World War I. At least three witnesses are needed for recommendation. All medals require royal assent and are presented by the reigning monarch. The inscription on front of the VC states simply: 'For Valour'.

LANCE CORPORAL WILLIAM COLTMAN

Of the 11 members of the Staffordshire Regiment awarded the VC, probably the most famous is Lance Corporal William Coltman, a stretcher bearer during operations at Mannequin Hill in France on 3 and 4 October, 1918. Hearing that wounded men had been left behind during a retreat, he went forward alone in the face of relentless enemy fire, found the casualties, dressed their wounds and carried some of them to safety on his back on three occasions. For the next two days and nights he looked after the wounded. He later became the most decorated NCO of World War I.

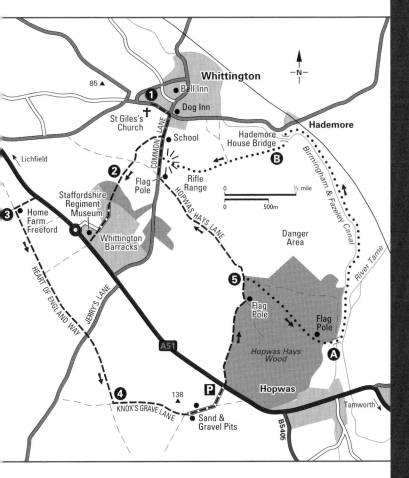

1 From St Giles's Church head into the village to a crossroads. Turn right for 250yds (229m) along Common Lane until you get to Sandy Lane. Turn right on this wide earth track until it bends hard right, and here go ahead through a gate and in the same direction to the corner of a wood.

2 Go through a swing gate and head slightly left through the wood, on a small brambly path, ignoring bigger paths setting off to left and right. At the residential tarmac road bear left to a wider road, and then right, to pass the Staffordshire Regiment Museum and go onto the A51. Turn right and walk along the pavement for 700yds (640m), passing a roundabout on the way. At South Lodge turn along a wide track to Home Farm Freeford.

3 Turn left onto the earth track of the Heart of England Way. Where a track joins from the left, move slightly right through a gate onto an enclosed grass track. Keep ahead for 0.75 miles (1.2km), through several gates and across a horse gallop, to a metalled road. Cross onto a hedged path, which passes a small square of trees on its right then crosses a farm track.

Another 500yds (457m) brings you to the junction with Knox's Grave Lane, a wide sandy track.

4 Turn left along here and then fork right at the top of a field to reach the corner of the sand and gravel pits. An abandoned tarmac road ahead threads between the pits on either side, down the dip and then up the other side. At the top of the rise, cross the stile on the left onto a field-edge alongside the gravel pit. At the far side of the field, cross a stile and the A51, and then go straight up the track to a T-junction. Turn left and follow the edge of Hopwas Hays Wood for 0.5 miles (800m). At a range flagpole, bear left to a major track junction at the corner of the wood.

5 From here follow the track of Hopwas Hays Lane ahead for another 0.5 miles (800m) onto the rifle range. Just across a small stream, bear right on a grass path across the firing range and up to a tarmac track leading to Common Lane. Turn right here, back towards Whittington and, at the crossroads, turn left to return to the start.

WHERE TO EAT AND DRINK The Bell Inn in Whittington serves a selection of bar snacks and main meals, lunchtimes and evenings. It also has a popular children's play area.

WHAT TO SEE The Coltman Trench, named after Lance Corporal William Coltman, is one of the highlights of the museum. The figures mentioned, however, are incomprehensible. On 1 July, 1916, the first day of the Battle of the Somme, 60,000 soldiers died in a single day. When the war ended on 11 November, 1918, more than 9 million people had been killed.

WHILE YOU'RE THERE The regimental chapel in Lichfield Cathedral (see Walk 42) features dozens of banners and colours from the regiment's long tradition of foreign campaigns. At the entrance is a stand surmounted by a figure of St George, which bears memorial books containing the names of men who fell in the World Wars.

Hopwas Hays Wood

DISTANCE 9 miles (14.5km)   MINIMUM TIME 3hrs 30min

ASCENT/GRADIENT 300ft (91m) ▲▲▲   LEVEL OF DIFFICULTY ✚✚✚

NOTE Firing range restrictions may apply, see note on Walk 43

SEE MAP AND INFORMATION PANEL FOR WALK 43

At Point ❺, turn hard right at the major 4-way junction, almost back on yourself, for a slightly sunken track up through the woodland. At the top bear right and stay straight along this wide dirt and gravel track, ignoring any smaller paths off to the left or right. The path drops through the woods to pass a range flagpole. Just keep following it round to the left as far as the bridge over the canal, Point ❹.

Cross the canal and turn left along the tow path. Walk for 1.75 miles (2.8km) to pass under Hademore House Bridge. In another 50yds (46m) turn right, up off the tow path. Return to the bridge and use it to cross over the tow path you already walked on and the canal. Continue straight ahead along a wide, sandy track for 100yds (91m) and then turn right along another sand track between

poly tunnels, as far as a gap between two hedges, Point ❸.

Go through the gap and continue in the same direction, with a hedge on your right, following a track and then a path until it goes between two hedges along a narrow dirt trail. At a T-junction with a wide track, turn left and then immediately right, along another narrow dirt trail to the right of a hedge.

Beyond an iron gate and a military firing range sign (see While You're There), follow the footpath sign to the right along the faint grass trail around the edge of the field, keeping the hedge on your right. Carry on to the far right-hand corner of this field where the hedge meets a small cottage and the metalled road (Common Lane) leading back into Whittington.

WHILE YOU'RE THERE If the red flags are flying, keep out! The area around Hopwas Hays Wood, marked by red triangles on Ordnance Survey maps, is a military firing range open to the public when it's not in use. Towards the end of the extension, just before you get to Common Lane, if you look back over your left shoulder you'll see the rifle range itself stretching 800yds (732m) to the target area at the far end. If that doesn't sound like a long way to shoot a high-powered rifle, try to imagine hitting any target smaller than a bus from this distance, while bearing in mind that sharp shooters can group six shots in an area smaller than a playing card.

Chasewater

DISTANCE 3 miles (4.8km)	**MINIMUM TIME** 1hr 15min

ASCENT/GRADIENT 75ft (23m) ▲▲▲   **LEVEL OF DIFFICULTY** ✚✚✚

PATHS Gravel tracks

LANDSCAPE Lakeside and heathland

SUGGESTED MAP OS Explorer 244 Cannock Chase

START/FINISH Grid reference: SK040071

DOG FRIENDLINESS Can be taken off lead

PARKING Ample parking at start point; follow signs 'Chasewater' off A6

PUBLIC TOILETS At Chasewater Innovation Centre

Originally Chasewater was a natural reservoir called Norton Pool, but little is known about its history prior to the late 18th century; with its poor acidic soil, heathland and forest, it was unsuitable for cultivation. But during the Napoleonic Wars (1803–15) there was a drive throughout the country to increase food production for the army, so areas of heathland and forest went under the plough.

CHASE THAT WATER SUPPLY

In 1797 a dam was constructed to turn the pool into a feeder reservoir for the Anglesey Branch Canal, newly built to carry coal from local pits to Birmingham and beyond. As the canal had little natural catchment, any extra water in winter was lifted back from the canal into the reservoir by a steam-driven pump. The valve house of this remains today, on top of the dam wall.

STEAM CARRIES COAL

With the arrival of the railways in the second half of the 19th century, canals were – quite literally – overtaken by the new technology. A network of tracks in the area included the causeway across the water, which carried coal from Cannock Chase. Mining around Chasewater continued well into the 20th century, but by 1950 it was an industry in decline, leaving a desolate landscape of disued railways, sidings and pit waste.

RESERVOIR LEISURE

Even back then, the local authority had the foresight to transform Chasewater into an aquatic pleasure park, complete with funfair, big wheel and miniature railway. The funfair is no more, but the park has recently undergone renovation and now features a waterskiing centre, as well as sailing and wind-surfing. For those who prefer their leisure pursuits a little more leisurely, there are displays at Chasewater Innovation Centre (free admission, open daily all year).

But the most significant achievement of the reclamation programme is its thriving wildlife. Today, much of the area has been designated as a Site of Special Scientific Interest (SSSI). In summer, when the water is low, the sediment along the shore makes an ideal feeding ground for birds such as herons, pied wagtails and ringed plovers. The stringy mat of weed over the exposed beaches is the rare but aptly named shoreweed. During winter, coots, mute swans and a vast roost of gulls are best watched from the south shore in late afternoon. Cormorants and Canada geese are also common, and great crested grebes can often be spotted displaying in spring. Some 230 different bird species have been noted here.

Heathland favours acid-loving plants; areas reclaimed from mining support only coarse grass and little in the way of wildlife. Natural grassland, though, boasts a rich variety of plants, such as lichens, mosses and cowslips. Finally, there are the bogs – disliked by walkers, but, as a habitat, appreciated by naturalists.

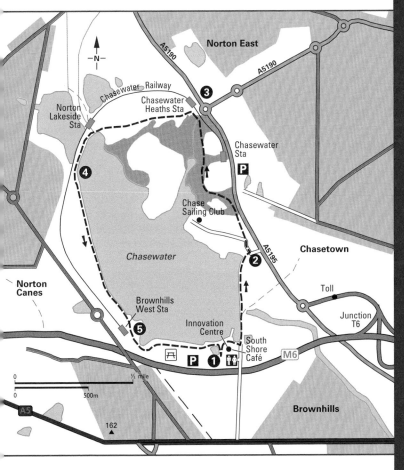

1 From the car park, go past the Innovation Centre and adjoining cafe down to the shore of the reservoir, and turn right. Bend left around the corner of the reservoir, and follow the tarmac path along the top of the concrete dam. At its end, drop to the right, off the path, to join the road running round to the left, towards Chase Sailing Club.

2 After 220yds (201m), as the road turns hard left, carry straight on along a wide gravel track, following cycle route signs. Keep following this track around, ignoring a path to the left, then forking left alongside the busy A5195 road. The wide path is sometimes gravel, sometimes tarmac. It passes to the left of some sports pitches, then bends right to pass alongside what looks like a pond but is in fact a corner of the reservoir. Finally it turns away from the reservoir, with a small stream on its left, to reach Chasewater Heaths Station.

3 Don't cross to the station, but stay on the wide tarmac path as it veers left, back towards the reservoir. It crosses open heath, to rejoin the railway at the start of its causeway across the north end of the reservoir. Turn left, alongside the railway, to cross the causeway.

4 Turn left on a wide dirt path along the shoreline. There are some carved picnic benches along this shoreline if you want to stop for a rest or a bite to eat, or just to watch the world go by. The sound of the steam train is carried across the water. The shoreline itself is reinforced by the roots of the tough willow trees that grow there.

5 The path becomes tarmac as you pass to the left of Brownhills West Station, then pass around to the right of the Chase Water Ski Centre at the reservoir corner. Bear left off the main tarmac path to join a well-made gravel one along the shoreline. This path even ventures out on decking across the water of a tiny bay, before arriving at a swan pond just in front of the Innovation Centre. Pass around (or through) the Innovation Centre to the car park.

WHERE TO EAT AND DRINK The South Shore Café, adjoining the Chasewater Innovation Centre, is open daily, all year round. It serves a range of snacks and light refreshments, including freshly made sandwiches and a salad bar. In the summer, you can take an ice cream out onto the waterfront.

WHAT TO SEE Boggy areas can be divided into two types: true bog, which supports sphagnum moss and acid-loving plants like cotton grass; and fen, which is alkaline and harbours reed mace and, in early to mid-summer, slender pink or white marsh orchids.

WHILE YOU'RE THERE Chasewater Railway operates along the only remaining section of the old Cannock Chase coalfield network. The steam-powered trips can be taken around the water from Brownhills West to Chasetown Station via Chasewater Heaths Station. The former has been built in traditional Victorian style and has a gift shop and a station buffet serving hot and cold snacks. The return trip takes an hour, with both diesel and steam-hauled trains running most weekends throughout the year. For more details go to www.chasewaterrailway.co.uk.

Trysull's Vineyard

DISTANCE 6.25 miles (10.1km)	**MINIMUM TIME** 2hrs 15min

ASCENT/GRADIENT 270ft (82m) ▲▲▲   **LEVEL OF DIFFICULTY** ✦✦✦

PATHS Roads, grass and dirt trails, gravel tracks

LANDSCAPE Village, farmland and escarpment top

SUGGESTED MAP OS Explorer 219 Wolverhampton & Dudley

START/FINISH Grid reference: SO852943

DOG FRIENDLINESS Keep on lead near livestock

PARKING Street parking in Trysull; also Hunters Green near village hall

PUBLIC TOILETS None on route

The Halfpenny Green Vineyards is situated on the southern-facing slopes of Upper Whittimere, to make the most of the sun throughout the year. The area was first planted in 1983 with the idea of producing wine for personal consumption, but the fine quality of the results led to it becoming a thriving business, and an astonishing 50,000 bottles are produced here every year.

IT BEGAN WITH THE ROMANS
The vineyard is one of more than 400 in the UK, most of them in the south of England or South Wales. Winemaking is enjoying something of a revival in this country, thanks largely to improved methods and a rigorous application of science in overcoming the problems of drought, disease and lack of sunshine. Since the Romans cultivated vines here almost 2,000 years ago numerous attempts have been made to make English vineyards a viable alternative to their continental counterparts, but almost without exception these efforts ended in failure.

THE BRITISH WEATHER
It wasn't until after World War II that research chemist Ray Barrington Brock set himself the mission of discovering which varieties of grape could cope best with the vagaries of the British weather. His work inspired others to follow suit, and in 1955 the first English wine to be made commercially since World War I went on sale.

Since then, there has been a steady increase in the number of vineyards and labels. In the last decade or so, however, this trend has levelled off, partly because many vineyards were established with little knowledge of the science involved. It has been said that the best way to earn a small fortune is to start with a large fortune and buy an English vineyard. Today though, there are numerous thriving vineyards throughout the south, despite the fact that in England only two years in every ten are 'good' years, with four average and four poor, again largely due to problems associated with weather. The most successful vineyards are well-sited with respect to sunlight and soil, grow appropriate varieties for the conditions, and are managed as scientific and commercial enterprises.

QUALITY WINES

Wines labelled as 'British' are made in the UK from imported wine concentrate and are usually of poor quality. To be labelled 'English', wines must be made from grapes grown in England, with the wine itself also made in England. Time was when turning one's nose up at English 'plonk' was justified, but if the wine at Halfpenny Green is anything to go by, domestic wine is now flowing more strongly than ever.

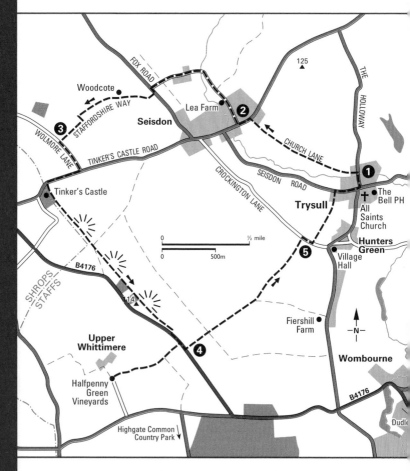

❶ From All Saints Church, head north along The Holloway for 100yds (91m) and, just after crossing a small brook, turn left along Church Lane. This soon becomes a farm track, then a hedged path that may be muddy after heavy rain. Emerging at Seisdon, turn left along the road (there is no pavement here, so exercise caution), and then take the first road on the right, Post Office Road.

2 Follow this road past Lea Farm all the way round to a T-junction with Fox Road. Turn left, then immediately right at a bridleway signpost. Follow this track past the crumbling sheds of Woodcote. At the top of the lane (Staffordshire Way marker), go through a swing gate to continue along a narrower dirt trail with a hedge to the left. At the corner of the hedge follow the path left around the edge of the field and then immediately right up to a metalled farm driveway, Wolmore Lane.

3 Turn left along this to a T-junction, then right along Tinker's Castle Road. At the top of the hill, just before Tinker's Castle house, head left up a path between a wall and a fence. The path runs ahead along the wooded ridge top for 1.25 miles (2km) to join the B4176. The road ahead continues the walk, but first, opposite the junction, head right along a wide field track (signed as a public footpath) to visit Halfpenny Green Vineyards (tea

room and restaurant, gift shop and craft centre). Return to the B4176 and (arriving from the vineyard) recross the road, then turn right along it for 50yds (46m), then turn off left at a footpath sign.

4 Go straight across the middle of the field to a stile, cross a track, then follow the hedge just to your right in the same direction. At the far right-hand corner of this field keep going straight on, aiming for a very large holly bush in the hedge ahead. Go through a wide gap in the hedge and bear slightly left on a faint field path, crossing the bank of a former hedge and down to a stile onto Crockington Lane. (If this field is impassable because of crops, you can bear right along the hedge to Fiershill Farm, but this means a longer walk along the road into Trysull.)

5 Turn right along Crockington Lane for 100yds (91m), before turning left through a kissing gate. Go straight on across this field to the far side and then down a track between houses to Seisdon Road. Turn right here, back to the start.

WHERE TO EAT AND DRINK The Bell in Trysull is an excellent village pub offering food at lunchtime and in the evening, every day. Bar snacks are served at very reasonable prices, and there's also a full restaurant menu. The interior is friendly and relaxed, while the picnic tables have a fine view of All Saints Church.

WHAT TO SEE As you walk along Wolmore Lane (Point **3**), check out the huge holly bushes that have got away from the hedge trimmer and formed themselves into trees. English holly can grow up to 50ft (15m) or higher. The male and female flowers are produced on different plants. In order for bees and other insects to pollinate female flowers and so form berries, male trees need to be planted within 100ft (30m) or so.

WHILE YOU'RE THERE Highgate Common Country Park, just to the south of Trysull, offers a wide expanse of open heathland and forest, with numerous trails criss-crossing the area and plenty of perfect picnic spots. There are public toilets at the southwest car park.

The Wombourne Railway Walk

DISTANCE 4.25 miles (6.8km)	**MINIMUM TIME** 1hr 30min

ASCENT/GRADIENT 360ft (110m) ▲▲▲   **LEVEL OF DIFFICULTY** ✦✦✦

PATHS Roads, gravel and dirt tracks

LANDSCAPE Disused railway, meadow and hilltop

SUGGESTED MAP OS Explorer 219 Wolverhampton & Dudley

START/FINISH Grid reference: SO870939

DOG FRIENDLINESS Must be on lead in fields and on roads

PARKING South Staffordshire Railway Walk car park, Bratch Lane, Wombourne

PUBLIC TOILETS None on route

Referred to in the Domesday Book as Womburne, Wombourne's name is thought to mean 'winding stream'. At that time (1086) it was reported as having a population of just 26 people, and by 1641 that number had barely risen above 100. It was not a booming town, and despite a number of small industries making their mark on the village in subsequent centuries – agriculture from the 1750s, horticulture around 1800, and sand-mining and nail production from about 1850 – it served as little more than a stop-off on the Staffordshire and Worcestershire Canal throughout this time.

THE CANALS...

The canal was one of the first to be built in Staffordshire, designed by engineering genius James Brindley (see Walk 50). It was well placed for the Potteries, carrying goods to and from Bristol, Gloucester and the West Country via the River Severn. Later, in the 1830s, it faced stiff competition from the Worcestershire and Birmingham Canal and the Birmingham and Liverpool Junction Canal, but still continued to make a profit until the 1860s. By then, however, the impact of the railways was beginning to bite, and the canal ceased to be a significant transport route by the turn of the century.

...AND THE RAILWAYS

As it turned out, the local railway fared little better, again thanks to competition from bigger, inter-city lines. The South Staffordshire Railway, serving the rural areas to the west of Dudley and Wolverhampton, was owned by Great Western Railways. Building started in 1912, but was not completed until 1925. Right from the start the line wasn't very successful, and passenger services were withdrawn by 1932. During World War II, following the D-Day landings in June

1944, it was used to transport wounded Allied soldiers to hospitals in the area, and after the war it was used for transporting goods.

Following the nationalisation of the railways in 1948, it became a part of the Western Region of what was then British Railways, but the decline in traffic during the 1950s and 1960s resulted in its closure. The rail company's loss was the public's gain. Today the old line has been converted into a popular walking and cycle path, the South Staffordshire Railway Walk, through quiet, rolling farmland, the flat, all-weather surface making it ideal for wheelchairs, pushchairs and family cycling. The route along the railway line can be extended in either direction by continuing along the Pensnett section in Dudley or the Valley Park section in Wolverhampton.

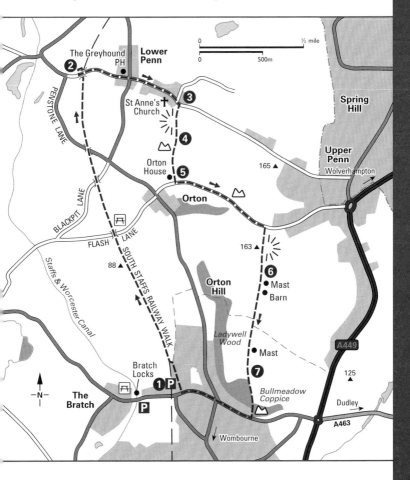

❶ From the far end of the car park, walk the few paces on to the disused South Staffordshire Railway line, beyond the former station and platform. Head right and continue along the gravel track for 1.5 miles (2.4km), passing over Flash Lane, Blackpit Lane and Penstone Lane (there are picnic benches near both Flash Lane and Blackpit Lane).

2 Immediately after the first bridge you go under, turn left up a short track to the road, and then head left over that same bridge and along the road for 0.5 miles (800m). It's usually quiet but there are one or two blind corners, so care needs to be taken. Pass The Greyhound pub in Lower Penn on your left, and continue over the crossroads towards Upper Penn.

3 Pass St Anne's Church and Rose Cottage on the right. Opposite a barn, take a gate on your right. A footpath sign indicates the path across the field to another kissing gate. Follow a grass path ahead across the next field to yet another kissing gate.

4 Through this gate go down some steep wooden steps and through a kissing gate. Continue down the steep, well-worn trail (this gets very slippery when wet) to reach the bottom of the field before crossing a stile. Stay on the narrow dirt track ahead; it might be thick with greenery in the summer, but there should be an obvious passage through.

5 At Orton House, turn left along the narrow, single-track road for 0.5 miles (800m); again, it's very quiet, but take care on blind bends. The road steepens up to the top. Just after the brow of the hill, turn right along a wide track (a public bridleway) past a wide house. This hedge-lined route offers great views of the rolling green hills of the Black Country to the east.

6 Follow the track as it passes to the right of the communications mast and a large concrete and steel barn. When the track goes hard left, cross a stile ahead and continue in the same direction across the middle of the field to the near end of Bullmeadow Coppice.

7 Turn down left for a few steps, then right on a path through a corner of the coppice to an open meadow. Ignore a path to the left; keep straight on along the wood edge to the field's corner. Here go right for a narrow path down the steep and sometimes slippery hillside. At the edge of Wombourne turn right along Bratch Lane and go straight over a crossroads to return to the car park at the start.

WHERE TO EAT AND DRINK If the weather's fine then there's no better place to have your lunch than at Bratch Locks picnic site, right by the canal. But those who travel on the railway should stop at the Station – the Railway Café at the walk start offers tea and crumpets, as well as lunch and even breakfast, plus a weekly walk every Thursday. It's closed on Mondays and after 3pm.

WHAT TO SEE Although Wombourne's 14th-century village church is of little interest architecturally, it's thought to be unique in its dedication to Saint Biscop, a Benedictine monk born in AD 628 and famed for the pictures and manuscripts he collected on his travels.

WHILE YOU'RE THERE Bratch Locks, on the Staffordshire and Worcestershire Canal just west of the start point, are well worth visiting. This three-tiered stair, negotiating a 30ft (9m) rise, is arguably the highlight of Brindley's canal. Two large side ponds were built to accept excess water diverted from the two upper locks.

Kinver's Rock Houses

DISTANCE 2.75 miles (4.4km)   **MINIMUM TIME** 1hr

ASCENT/GRADIENT 374ft (114m) ▲▲▲   **LEVEL OF DIFFICULTY** ✚✚✚

PATHS Wide gravel tracks and dirt paths

LANDSCAPE Woodland and escarpment top

SUGGESTED MAP OS Explorer 219 Wolverhampton & Dudley

START/FINISH Grid reference: SO835836

DOG FRIENDLINESS Can be taken off lead

PARKING Verge car park on Compton Road, Kinver

PUBLIC TOILETS None on route

The sandstone ridge to the southwest of Kinver has been occupied in one way or another since 2500 BC, and impressive earthworks, believed to have been built around this time, still exist near the summit.

KINVER EDGE

The views from the summit, and along the length of Kinver Edge, are tremendous, and it must have seemed an impressive vantage point on which to build defences. Today, a brass relief map at the north end (Point ❷), points to some of the world's major capitals, as well as less distant landmarks. The Malvern Hills, 30 miles (48km) to the south, and Long Mynd, the same distance to the west, are visible on a clear day and it may be possible to see the Black Mountains, over 45 miles (72km) away. But for all its breathtaking views, the real interest lies below the summit, in small houses carved into the rock.

HOLY AUSTIN ROCK

Of these, by far the most impressive are the dwellings at Holy Austin Rock, east of the car park. Legend has it that it was named after a hermit who lived near the site. The first written reference to people actually living in houses cut out of the rock face is believed to be in a book about a walk in the area, written in 1777.

FAMILY HOMES

By the beginning of the 19th century there were several rock houses, and for the next 100 years or so they were permanently occupied. By 1861 there were 11 families in residence, the increase almost certainly due to the demand created by the local iron works. When these went into decline at the end of the 19th century, the houses were abandoned, although two families continued to live there until the end of World War II, and the last occupants didn't move out until 1963. A tourist cafe lasted until 1967, after which the houses fell into decline and neglect: vandalism led to collapses and one area had to be destroyed for safety reasons. In the 1980s plans were drawn up to renovate the houses to their original state. The rebuilding was completed in 1993 and the site was occupied by a National Trust custodian. While this house is private, the rest of the site is open during daylight hours all year round. The interiors of lower rock houses are open on weekend afternoons from March to the end of November (2–4pm). Visitors may be surprised at just how cosy the houses feel.

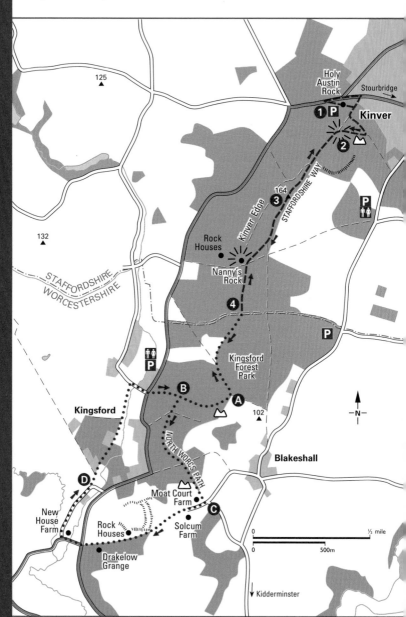

1 From the wide roadside car parking, head back along the road towards Kinver village. Just after going right at a fork in the road, follow public footpath signs to the right, up a short track into the woods. Once you're in the woods proper, take the obvious path up left to a small clearing and then turn 90 degrees to the right to follow the short, steep path to the viewpoint above Kinver.

2 From the viewpoint, continue along the top of the escarpment, following a wide, gravel track running more or less along the uphill edge of the ancient rectangular earthworks to the left, with views across the Severn Valley glimpsed through trees to the right. From the corner of the earthworks, continue on the wide and well-walked track through intermittent woodland, with new and distant views opening up on either side. Carry on along the escarpment top, to pass the trig point.

3 Staying on the highest path, continue for 0.25 miles (400m), when the path enters woodland.

In 60yds (55m), just after a path joins from the left, a steep path down to the right is marked 'danger cliff edge'. Following this down for about 40yds (37m) would take you to Nanny's Rock. The main route descends gradually to the gate at the National Trust boundary before a small clearing. Here a signpost for the Staffordshire Way (back towards you) and the North Worcestershire Path (ahead) marks the county boundary. A narrow track to the right leads back down to the road and a public toilet if required, although it criss-crosses other paths and it's very easy to lose your bearings!

4 For this reason, it's easiest to return the way you came. From the clearing at the county boundary, head back along the escarpment to the viewpoint. At the end, head right and then left, back down to the clearing, and then left again down the wooden steps, through the trees to the short track above the road. Here a gate up on the left leads to the Rock Houses. Explore the site, then follow the path past the lower rock houses down to the car park.

WHERE TO EAT AND DRINK The Tea Rooms at the Holy Austin Rock houses continue the tradition of 1777, in the top level of houses, with rock-carved back rooms. They are open from Thursday to Sunday, 11am–4pm.

WHAT TO SEE Nanny's Rock, just below the path, provides an exciting viewpoint and a great place for a picnic. Continue down past it on the steep and somewhat rocky path (take care here) then turn right on a wider path to reach a set of simple carved-out cave dwellings. Like Nanny's Rock above, they are heavily graffitised by amateur rock carvers – what will the geologists of future eras make of these 'trace fossils'?

Overleaf: Nanny's Rock, Kinver Edge (Walks 48 and 49)

The Worcestershire Loop

DISTANCE 6 miles (9.7km)   **MINIMUM TIME** 2hrs 15min

ASCENT/GRADIENT 750ft (229m) ▲▲▲   **LEVEL OF DIFFICULTY** +++

SEE MAP AND INFORMATION PANEL FOR WALK 48

From Point ❹, continue along the escarpment. Keep to the main (higher) track and follow waymarkers for the North Worcestershire Path. The path turns down left around a small covered reservoir, then turns back up to the ridge crest. Turn left, down to the corner of an open field (Point ❹).

Turn right, past a barrier and a bench, to descend a fairly steep path. Where this path meets a wooden barrier and a more obvious sand track at right angles, Point ❸, head left, gently uphill. After 300yds (274m) you come to another path junction. Bear left onto the smallest, central path, following the yellow arrow. On reaching a sandy track go straight over, coming shortly to a steep hill. When you get to the top, cross a stile and continue along the field-edge, with a fence to your left. In the far left corner of the field, go through a gate onto the road (Point ❸).

Turn right (marked No Through Road), passing Moat Court Farm on the right and, shortly after, keep to the right of Solcum Farm following a yellow arrow down a dark and heavily wooded track. As you descend into the dark woods, the steep bank to the right forms the remains of some Iron Age earthworks not unlike the ones at the start of the walk. After a brick shed on the right, look up right to spot another group of cave houses, these ones far less developed than the ones at Holy Austin Rock. The earth path emerges onto a concrete track past the recently built, half-timbered Drakelow Grange. At the road junction beyond, continue straight on and take the first right at New House Farm. Carry on to where the surfaced road turns to the right, Point ❶.

Here follow the tarmac track bearing left, in a few steps taking the right fork. At the end of the houses, when the track turns up, continue straight on to the right of a fence, following the yellow arrows with a stream on your right. A gate leads onto the tarmac lane below Kingsford Farm. Turn down right until it meets a bigger road. Go straight across and up a footpath just to the left, by a Forest Park sign. When this path meets a wide sandy bridleway (Point ❸ again), continue across and back up the way you came, retracing your steps back to Point ❹.

Kinver to Whittington

DISTANCE 3.25 miles (5.3km)   MINIMUM TIME 1hr 15min

ASCENT/GRADIENT 360ft (110m) ▲▲▲   LEVEL OF DIFFICULTY ✦✦✦

PATHS Grass tracks, field paths, roads and dirt trails, many stiles

LANDSCAPE Field, meadow, woodland and canalside

SUGGESTED MAP OS Explorer 219 Wolverhampton & Dudley

START/FINISH Grid reference: SO848835

DOG FRIENDLINESS Keep on lead in all fields

PARKING At Kinver Lock (walk start); Kinver High Street

PUBLIC TOILETS Kinver High Street

Given the part canals have played in the Staffordshire landscape over the past 250 years, it seems appropriate that the final walk in the book should include at least a short section of artificial waterway, even if it isn't the walk's highlight. It seems fitting too, that the Staffordshire and Worcestershire Canal was designed and built under the apparently omnipotent eye of James Brindley, whose name is associated with so many of the walks in this volume, and who perhaps did more than any other single person to shape the landscape and fortune of the county.

WATERWAY TO GO

The Staffordshire and Worcester Canal was one of Brindley's earliest projects; it was officially opened in 1772. Essentially, it was part of his so-called 'Grand Cross', a visionary scheme to connect all of the major ports (Bristol, Hull and Liverpool) by linking the Severn, the Trent and the Mersey. The canal begins at the River Severn before rising slowly to Aldersley Junction, near Wolverhampton, where it connects with the Shropshire Union Canal (see Walk 35). It then continues as far as the Trent and Mersey Canal at Great Haywood near Shugborough (see Walk 33). Its highlight has to be the three-tier lock at The Bratch, near Wombourne (see Walk 47).

TURN IN HERE WHITTINGTON

Despite James Brindley's best efforts, the highlight of this walk has to be the Whittington Inn, a timber-beamed manor house built in 1310 that now serves a very reasonable pint – and also has a handy selection of spirits. It was originally owned by Sir William de Whittington, then lord of Kinver and grandfather of Dick Whittington, who became Lord Mayor of London.

SHADES OF GREY

The house was later inherited by ancestors of Lady Jane Grey, who spent some of her childhood here, before her life was plunged into turmoil. She was fourth in line to the throne in Henry VIII's will, but thanks to the scheming of her Protestant father-in-law, a royal advisor, she was crowned Queen ahead of Henry's daughter Mary, who was Catholic. She ruled for just nine days, before Mary, with strong popular support, seized the throne and had her imprisoned in the Tower of London. Less than a year later, aged just 16, she was beheaded. During the reign of Mary's successor, Queen Elizabeth I, Jane was celebrated as a Protestant martyr. Today, her ghost is said to still haunt the inn staircase. Meanwhile, the shade of Dick Whittington has been spotted, in a black coach galloping soundlessly south towards Kidderminster.

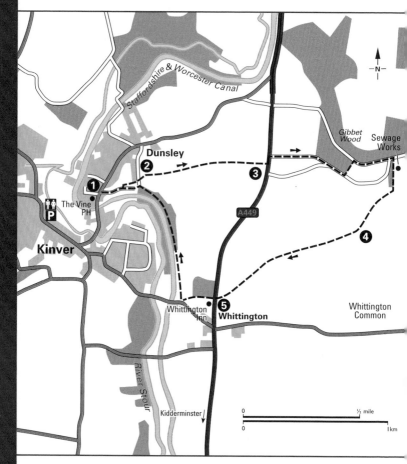

1 From The Vine pub beside Kinver Lock, go up Dunsley Road for 100yds (91m) and turn right along a gravel track ('Gibraltar') between houses. In 200yds (183m) bear left up a fairly steep path through woods to the corner of a driveway. Turn up left, and then right just after Dunsley House, along a short dirt and grass track.

2 At the track's end keep ahead over a stile, with a tall cupressus hedge on your right (it protects a small vineyard). Continue straight ahead from stile to stile across one small field, then down over another small one and two very large ones to a final stile onto the A449.

3 Take care crossing this fast, busy road, then head left for 110yds (100m) to a stile. Follow the fenced path next to newly planted trees up to the corner of Gibbet Wood. Turn right, following the edge of the wood around to a stile on the left, and then up the wood edge to a rough track, Gibbet Lane. Turn right here for 350yds (320m) and right again over a stile in a high metal fence. Once across the private access road, head down the left edge of the next field. At its foot turn right along a tree-lined track.

4 At the track end, continue along a fence to your right for 100yds (91m). As the fence bears round to the right, keep going straight on, past a brick pedestal and a lonely stile mid-field, then slightly up over a brow to find a stile beyond. Bear slightly left down the next field to a stile (a gate is on its left), and then cut off the corner of the next field to cross a stile, one more small field, and a stile with a gate alongside. Follow the top, left-hand edge of this final large field all the way to a stile onto the A449 opposite the Whittington Inn.

5 Cross the busy road here (taking great care) and pass to the right of the inn (footpath sign to Lower Whittington). A small path along an ivy-covered wall leads to a hedged way down between houses to a road corner. Turn right, following a footpath sign, to a field beside the canal. Follow its bank along the field, through some woods and below some canal-front houses. Just after them, fork right, uphill, to the driveway corner passed before Point **2** on the outward walk. Bear down left back to Kinver Lock.

WHERE TO EAT AND DRINK The Whittington Inn is the obvious place to feast and imbibe, either during the walk or afterwards. Home-cooked food and real ale are served in cosy, immaculate (and ancient) surroundings, all day. Dogs are allowed in the beer garden only.

WHAT TO SEE The 14th-century front door of the Whittington Inn bears a metal disc alongside the handle: this is Queen Anne's seal, with the inscription 'Anne R. 1711', indicating that she stayed here on one of her royal trips. It's thought that this is one of only two of her seals in existence.

WHILE YOU'RE THERE The Red House Glass Cone museum at Stourbridge is an industrial remnant sitting alongside a branch of the same strategic canal system. The very striking building, 100ft (30m) high and built around 1790, is made of brick (rather than glass) and acted not just as the housing, but also the chimney of the glass furnace within. It's open daily, 10am–4pm, with glass-blowing demonstrations on Saturday and Sunday afternoons.

Titles in the Series